CONVENT GIRL
The Cross and The Lily

'In the Footsteps of Sarah Bernhardt'
Reminiscences of life at a Convent Boarding School during the 1940's.

CONVENT GIRL
The Cross and The Lily

'In the Footsteps of Sarah Bernhardt'
Reminiscences of life at a Convent Boarding School
during the 1940's.

By

Jean Barbara Bancroft

AVON BOOKS
1 DOVEDALE STUDIOS
465 BATTERSEA PARK ROAD
LONDON SW11 4LR

Printed and bound in the U.K.

Avon Books

London
First Published 1995
© Jean Barbara Bancroft 1995
ISBN 1 86033 141 6

DEDICATION

To the Canonesses of St. Augustine of the Congregation of Our Lady and to their former pupils the world over.

May their spirit live on!

Contents

The Cross And The Lily

An Education For Life

'To give it to them more fruitfully, the best, the surest and the most fitting way is this: By women in a congregation, striving to lead good lives, giving a free education, teaching goodness, and, at the same time, other things which of their nature can bring some temporal profit to those who learn them.'

(St Pierre Fourier, founder of the Canonesses of St Augustine of the Congregation of Our Lady, writing in 1627 of the importance of giving girls a Christian education.)

'To do all the good possible'
(Alix le Clerc)

'Nemini obesse, omnibus prodesse'
('Do harm to none, do good to all')

PREFACE

Living a Legend

How many Convent schoolgirls can boast of a headmistress who sat in a tree to read her breviary? The eccentricities of the nuns who brought us up are now legendary among us, but as pupils at Boynton we were brought up on the legend of Grand-Champs, the convent at Versailles very much in vogue from which the nuns had come to Hull at the beginning of the twentieth century, and where the great actress, Sarah Bernhardt, had been educated.

In the history of the Order that famous (and notorious) actress has been probably their most celebrated pupil. The fact that she was so happy at school is significant, underlying the reason for our own happiness amongst the nuns.

In her biography of Bernhardt, Ruth Brandon relates that Sarah 'was happier during her years at Grand-Champs than she had ever been. For the first time in her life she was settled and secure, and the prospect of a life with solid foundations opened up before her...Sarah loved the convent. She loved the kindly nuns, and she knew they loved her; she especially adored the Mother Superior, mère Sainte-Sophie, with her short, round figure, her laughing face and big blue eyes, her charm, her smile which "lit up the whole convent", and her great kindness and understanding. This was the kind of mother she had dreamed of but never had: she idolised mère Sainte-Sophie and never forgot her..."When I heard that I wasn't going back to the convent," wrote Sarah, "it seemed to me that I had been thrown into the sea, and I didn't know how to swim." ' [1]

In 1944, a hundred years after the birth of the legendary actress, as a new girl I too was to experience a period of security at the convent and, along with others of the pupils, began in some measure to walk in her footsteps (without achieving her greatness!) for there were aspects of her life with which I, at least, am able to identify; one of us, certainly, will have slept in the bed that she formerly occupied. I was not then to know that first Boynton, then the French Convent in Hull and finally Rise Convent were, like Grand-Champs, destined also to pass into the realm of legend.

Legend is often thought of as being part fact, part fiction. The following account contains historical fact, unadulterated, unexaggerated and uninhanced either by a false, retrospectively romantic sentimentality or by sensationalism. The account of our schooldays is justly complimentary, but there were aspects that were by no means perfect (and one at least that at the time could have been described as sensational!)

Former pupils at Hull, Boynton and Rise have lived what has now become legend and, like the illustrious former Old Girl of Grand-Champs, under the kindly nuns we found security and happiness and received a sure foundation for growth, a foundation that nurtured and encouraged spirituality and individuality, and which far from crushing our spirit directed it along the right lines.

In the figure of Mère Sainte-Sophie my contemporaries will recognise a combination of Mother Philomena, Mother Hilda and Mother AElfreda, but all the nuns will be remembered by us with great and lasting affection.

My own association with the Canonesses of St Augustine sprang, like the Order, from small beginnings. In October 1931, I was taken as a week old baby to the French Convent in Park Grove, Hull, to be introduced to the nuns. I have a fleeting memory of being placed in the arms of a figure in black at the bottom of the oak staircase (a memory that few people are willing to believe.) My sister, Dorothy, a former pupil of the French Convent and sixteen years older than I, had left school three months previously and was inordinately proud of me; she lost no time in taking the new baby to show to the nuns.

That association has continued to the present day, first through the education I received at Boynton and then at Rise, later through a period of teaching at Rise and then at the French Convent, and over the latter years through the twice yearly Reunions of the Old Girls' Association. In between times there have been constant visits to the Convent that I had come to regard almost as a second home.

The vicissitudes encountered during the war years, when the number of pupils dwindled considerably, were steadily counteracted once the boarders moved to Rise Hall; there the school gradually began to flourish again. This was due almost entirely to the vision and determination of one nun in particular. It was through the efforts of Mother AElfreda, later to become Headmistress and then Superior, that Rise Convent School obtained a reputation for excellence. In many ways, the name of Rise stands as a memorial to her.

Many schools have excellent reputations, but the French Convent first at Park Grove, and then at Boynton Hall and Rise possessed a quality that I believe to be unique, one that was directly responsible for the loyalty and happy atmosphere it engendered among the pupils and teachers there. Much has been written or told about Convent Schools, not all of it complimentary, but former pupils of the Canonesses of St Augustine rarely have had anything but good to say of the happy times they spent with the nuns.

In 1989 the school at Rise, like very many Convent Schools, regrettably had to close down, but Rise Convent continued to remain in being as a flourishing Conference, Retreat and Course Centre. September 1996 would have seen the celebration of its Golden Jubilee; unfortunately it has with great sorrow been decided to terminate the lease a few months earlier and to move into smaller premises. However, Rise and the Convent will always remain in the hearts of former pupils. In the following pages I hope the reason for this will gradually become apparent, although the account of the hardships of life at Boynton may initially make it hard for people nowadays to believe that we could have been so happy at school!

This account of my own schooldays in the 1940's has been written in gratitude for the education I received and as a tribute to the unique spirit of the Order that was founded in Lorraine, almost four hundred years previously, by St Pierre Fourier and Blessed Alix le Clerc. It is written also in happy memory of the nuns with whom I grew up, all but one of whom have since died, of my own schoolfriends and those of my sister at Park Grove, and in appreciation of the easy rapport that exists between fellow Old Girls of all ages.

We all have varying memories of our schooldays; I can only recount my own, but pupils of the Canonesses of St Augustine the world over will be able to relate to many of them and will have their own individual reminiscences in addition. For all of them the Cross and the Lily will have a special significance.

J.B.B.

November 1994

[1] Ruth Brandon, *Being Divine: a Biography of Sarah Bernhardt*

INTRODUCTION

In September 1946, at the start of a new school year, an observer would have noticed groups of schoolgirls leaning over the balconies of the adjacent halls below them, where furniture and other household items had been piled. At the same time fascinated and saddened by the poignancy of what was happening, they listened to the Auctioneer and watched as family heirlooms were disposed of under his hammer.

The former home of the Bethel family was being turned into a school. Old Mrs Bethel had died, and the heir, Richard Bethel, Lady Jane and the children, were already living in the former vicarage next to the main drive.

Family ancestors, looking down on the scene from their portraits which lined the walls of the grand staircase, could never have envisaged that the stately Georgian mansion would ever ring to the sounds of lively schoolchildren. They would have been even more astounded, and probably shocked, at the chanting of nuns, the murmurings of a Catholic Mass or the singing of Latin hymns emanating from the former Blue Drawing Room. For the Bethel family of Rise Park, near the East Yorkshire coastal resort of Hornsea, it was the end of an era; for the Canonesses of St.Augustine and their small number of pupils it was the beginning of a new one.

The war was over, the school had moved from Boynton, the vicarage became Rise Park and the Bethel family seat was renamed Rise Hall. It was to be a Convent Boarding School.

We had moved from Boynton Hall to Rise reluctantly, for we had loved our former school, but there was no going back. Life was to change, undoubtedly for the better in most respects, but nostalgic memories remain.

My own memories of life at Boynton are vivid, perhaps because I began life there as a boarder at an impressionable age and at a time of personal upheaval. For me it had been a new beginning and Rise represented a progression from that. To understand progression one needs, of course, to go back in time...

Chapter One

In September 1946 I had become a 'Rise Girl', one of a small army of pioneers, but my Convent schooling began in 1944, two and a half years earlier, and the beginning may not at first seem to have been very auspicious.

I was sent to boarding school at the age of twelve. My father had died when I was not yet five; I had been evacuated at the age of eight, first to Flamborough for a year and then to Halifax for almost four years; now, once again I had to adjust to major change and a new environment.

Early in 1944 I left behind the safety of the life I had become used to in the West Riding in order to return to East Yorkshire where I had been born. The war was not yet over and I was not allowed to remain in Hull and attend Newland High School as I had hoped, and for which I had passed what was then known as the Scholarship. Providence, in the person of my mother, decreed that I should go to the French Convent as a boarder at Boynton Hall near Bridlington, the country house which had been rented by the nuns in 1934 and to which the boarders had been evacuated at the outbreak of war in 1939. In the space of twelve years my life had been repeatedly disrupted: I had lived in three different households, had attended four different schools and now I was to attend a fifth one. Left to sink or swim, a precarious carpet pulled from under my feet, it was up to me to make the best of it. Fortunately, I learnt metaphorically to swim, but at the time my self-confidence took a plummeting; thin, lanky and with buck teeth, at the onset of adolescence and in a strange environment I felt awkward and self-conscious. All in all I didn't have much going for me!

The French Convent was not an entirely unknown quantity as my sister, sixteen years older than I, had been educated there, but that was at Park Grove in Hull, commandeered in the war by the army, and apart from having been taken there by Dorothy once or twice when I was very small I was not really familiar with it; I was certainly totally unfamiliar with Catholicism. This time I was to be truly thrown in at the deep end in spite of tenuous links with the nuns.

Having returned to Hull from Halifax I remained there for only as long as it took to buy my new school uniform, stitch on name tapes and pack the black old-fashioned trunk that had belonged to my mother. The blitz-ravaged town centre was almost unrecognisable, there were gaps where houses had once stood in Desmond Avenue where we lived, our house had suffered damage from bomb blasts and it seemed much smaller than I had remembered it to be: everything looked drab. At Halifax I had been physically sheltered from the worst aspects of wartime Britain, and had grown used to a country life. I had known the companionship of living with children of around my own age, life in the household of my aunt and uncle had been happy, relaxed and full of fun, controlled but not over-disciplined; my aunt had been a colourful presence, both in personality and appearance, and the family atmosphere had been a happy one. On returning to Hull I found I had little in common with my former friends, and mother and Dorothy had built up lives in which I had no real part to play. I had looked forward to my homecoming and felt let down, insecure and depressed.

In spite of natural apprehension, the prospect of boarding school life began to have some appeal, especially if it was going to live up to expectations fed by the 'Dimsie' books that my cousins and I had avidly read. At least there would surely be midnight feasts. As it turned out, being sent to the Convent proved to be a major turning point in my life and, in spite of vicissitudes and spartan conditions that might cause a modern child to quail, I was extremely happy at school.

Chapter Two

My first sight of the Elizabethan Hall, formerly the home of the Strickland family, was from the windows of a taxi as it entered the long, straight drive at the bottom end of Boynton village. We passed over a small bridge below which ran a stream called the Gypsy Race, and drew up at the red brick mansion that has since become legendary with former pupils. There were no other girls about: the term had already begun and they had been sent for a walk. Mother and I were met by the Headmistress, Mother Hilda, who had formerly taught my sister; we were taken to the Breakfast Room which served as a parlour, where Mother Hilda attempted to assess my academic ability, and then we were shown the Big Dormitory where I was to sleep. Mother departed in the waiting taxi and I was left feeling like Ruth amid the alien corn.

I was painfully shy and felt truly out of my depth; the only life-raft was the prospect of soon being able to see Mother Dorothea, the nun who had received me into her arms when I was a week old, who had been Dorothy's favourite teacher and whom I had been taken to see once or twice before the war.

I was deposited in a large, stone-flagged hall, on one side of which was a massive stone fireplace surrounded by a tall, wire fireguard. A log fire was burning in the grate and by the side of it sat an attractive young woman darning socks. Her name was Dot Oxley and she had been at school with my sister; she invited me to sit beside her.

Dot, whose husband was in the RAF, was one of the paying guests who had come to live at Boynton Hall when war broke out; her two young children, Jacquie and Nigel, attended the school in the class that was referred to as 'the babies'. In the absence of

Mother Dorothea I was glad to find some sort of link with home. Shy though I was, I tentatively offered to help Dot with her mending by sewing on buttons. No doubt I sewed them on badly but it helped to pass what seemed like a very long hour; she must have found making conversation with a tongue-tied, gawky twelve-year old rather a strain.

Relief came when the other pupils returned from their Sunday afternoon walk and I was surrounded by curious and friendly schoolgirls. We went into the Refectory for tea and I was given my first taste of boarding school food in the shape of bread and margarine.

The Refectory was a long, rectangular room opposite the Breakfast Room and was hung with portraits. In one corner was a 'tuck' cupboard and at the far end I believe there was another cupboard in which each pupil kept her own jar of jam, marmite or peanut butter (embellishments not supplied by the school) with which to make the bread and margarine more palatable.

I remember little of that first teatime, except the feeling of apprehension when one of the girls asked the nun in charge if there was a spare white veil for me to wear for Benediction. What was Benediction and why would I need a veil? Born and brought up in the middle rung of the Church of England, I had no knowledge of Catholicism except that services were held in Latin; it was as foreign to me as Hinduism. A white veil was produced and after tea we were lined up to go into the chapel, a rectangular room on the first floor overlooking the long South Lawn. I have no recollection of my first experience of Benediction but subconsciously it made an impression on me and I came to love Catholic ritual.

Mother Dorothea did not materialize and in answer to my questions I was told that she had gone away. It was a bitter disappointment and further questioning was met by evasion; there was an air of mystery that I couldn't fathom and it was only much later, after leaving school, that I learnt the reason for that. For some time she had been regularly driving to Bridlington when the other nuns were tucked up in bed, had changed into mufti and gone dancing with the soldiers stationed there. As usually happens, her sins found her out for she was eventually recognised and her misdemeanours reported to the powers that be! The scandal connected with her departure was at the time extremely damaging to the Convent, although nowadays it would probably have passed as a nine-day wonder. Her loss was also a bitter blow to the school, for she had been a brilliant teacher. I myself felt personally bereaved: I had been counting so much on being loved and welcomed by her.

At bedtime I was initiated into the complexities of undressing beneath my dressing-gown and of washing in an enamel bowl in the draughty corridor that served as a washroom. I also learnt that talking in the dormitory was strictly forbidden and that fresh air was considered to be the best means of keeping us healthy: the dormitory, which had a door opening on to the drive, was on the ground floor and we were made to sleep with the door to the outside world wide open, even on the coldest nights. I quickly discovered why all the girls spread their dressing-gowns over their beds! I was already inured to the miseries of homesickness but I did have to learn to endure real physical discomfort. All told, my introduction to boarding school life had been quite a shock to the system.

Chapter Three

Of my generation possibly only boys who were sent to Public Schools will be able to relate to the physical hardships we experienced at Boynton. We were always cold in winter and suffered perpetually from chilblains. The Hall was draughty and the central heating system archaic; every spare moment was spent huddled around a fire or sitting on the high, rounded radiators. Fires were lit in the main hall and in the classrooms but the dormitory was icy. Although modesty decreed that we undressed beneath our dressing-gowns, the rule was in fact a blessing, for disrobing under arctic conditions was not conducive to flaunting near nakedness. Warm dressing-gowns were retained until the last moment before we jumped into bed between icy sheets. We were allowed hot water bottles, which we filled from the hot water tap, but more often than not the water was only lukewarm.

Bedtime was at eight-thirty (six-thirty for the 'babies') and remained so for the rest of the time that I spent at the convent; and the Catholics had to rise at six-thirty in the morning for seven o'clock daily Mass, although the rest of us were allowed an extra half-hour in bed. The beds had been brought over from Grand-Champs, the school in the Rue Royale at Versailles from which the nuns had been obliged to flee in 1904 because of renewed anticlericalism, and were very comfortable; this, of course, made rising on cold mornings all the harder.

The Big Dormitory was housed in the former library. The original, leather-bound books were still there on the shelves around the walls, and the stark clinical appearance of the rows of white counterpaned beds contrasted sharply with the warm mellowness of volumes which had been there since Elizabethan times.

The Dormitory was strictly functional; there were no chairs or lockers by the beds. The beds themselves had white painted iron frames and at the end of each one hung the regulatory gas-mask case, one of the few reminders, together with rationing and clothes coupons, that there was still a war on. The counterpanes were wrapped round the pillows in the French manner.

Somewhat incongruously the neatness and uniformity was softened by the cuddly toy or pyjama case each child was allowed to place on her bed during the day, a fact that had impressed my mother and was in keeping with the spirit of the Order to which the nuns belonged: one in which discipline was tempered with kindness. The founder, St Peter Fourier, had insisted that his nuns should be as mothers to their pupils and treat them with understanding and gentleness. This would have been all very well had the two Matrons been as gentle and understanding as the nuns!

Close to the inner door of the dormitory was the white-curtained bed occupied by Mère Marie de l'Enfant Jesus, the French nun known to generations of schoolgirls and to the Community as Loffy. It was her unenviable task to keep us in order and try to enforce the rule of silence. After threatening us numerous times she would finally be driven to saying the dreaded words, 'You 'ave your Order Mark.' On Monday mornings at Assembly Order Marks, together with Merit Marks, received during the previous week were read out and we each had to confess to the particular crimes we had committed; the 'crime' was invariably that of talking in the refectory or the dormitory. I often wonder why 'punitive' methods of keeping order are so frowned upon these days; it certainly did us no harm to be humbled occasionally, and it gave added incentive to try hard to obtain Merit Marks for good schoolwork which would counteract the Order Marks when House totals for the week were read out.

It was not until many years later, long after I had left school, that the nuns were finally brought to see how unreasonable it was to expect modern children to conform to the religious life 'en miniscule' that had been the school pattern since the foundation of the Order in 1597. Like the nuns, we had to keep the 'Grand Silence'; we also had to spend a large part of mealtimes without talking and were not allowed to speak when lining up outside the Refectory or Chapel. Officially the nuns were 'enclosed' and this rule meant that to a certain extent the peace of the Cloister was maintained, but we were high-spirited children, not cloistered nuns, and such a régime resulted in constant breaking of the rule and numerous Order Marks, and must have driven Loffy almost to despair. It resulted also in the invention of ingenious ways of circumventing the rule, such as sticking our heads outside the window or up the chimney in order to talk to one another ('No, Mother, I wasn't talking in the dormitory!') The Jesuits had nothing over us when it came to casuistry!

The Catholics had an even harder time of it than the rest of us, being required to go to daily Mass along with the nuns and to Confession once a week; it gave a firm spiritual basis to their lives but they didn't find it easy! However, in vindication of the nuns, I am not aware of any of my Catholic contemporaries having since abandoned their religion.

Another irksome rule, eventually abolished, was the rest period we were made to spend in our beds for an hour after lunch at weekends. We hated it! The last thing healthy and energetic schoolgirls needed was to be put to bed for an hour during the day in a cold dormitory, even though we were allowed to read a book, especially as the silence rule was still enforced.

Immediately after 'rest' we were taken by Loffy for a compulsory walk. Wearing gabardines and outdoor shoes or Wellingtons, navy berets, scarves and woollen gloves, we tramped along lanes and through woods in all weathers and lagged behind whenever we could; occasionally we used the ploy of stopping to tie a shoelace and waiting until the others were out of sight before thankfully making our way back to school.

Those of us who were at Boynton can surely claim to have been among the nation's first joggers. Long before the English became obsessed with physical fitness, authority in the name of the Matron in charge of us decreed one day that henceforth all the pupils should go for a morning run. Each day after breakfast we were required to run down the path at the side of the long South Lawn and back again, whilst she and the Matron in charge of the 'babies' and the linen (who was commonly known as Maggie Lee) eyed us from the comfort of the Breakfast Room. The fact that they were eating toast by a blazing fire whilst we were forcibly exposed to the elements added insult to injury; however, we soon learnt to run past the Breakfast Room window, halt a few yards out of sight further on, wait for an appropriate length of time and then run past the window again. We knew we were safe from the eyes of the nuns who were then in chapel chanting their Morning Office.

Despite woollen gloves and the mittens that most of us wore indoors, my fingers were always frozen, numb with the cold, and we all suffered agonies from chilblains. After the morning run we had to return to the dormitory and make our beds which had been previously stripped. The white counterpanes had to be put over the beds in regulation manner with the corners neatly tucked in and folded at the bottom end and the pillow folded in at the top. We were never allowed to get away with a rushed job; whilst we were at breakfast Matron would have been in the dormitory in order to fling to the floor the blankets of any unstripped bed her eagle eyes rested upon, and once lessons began she would inspect the dormitory again to see that everything conformed to standard. The first lesson of the day was frequently interrupted by her entrance and the hauling out of culprits to remake their beds.

The cold was always with us. I have little recollection of warm summers at Boynton, certainly not when we were inside the building, for the dormitory and most of the classrooms faced north. The cold could have been endured more easily if the food we were given could have generated bodily heat; unfortunately it was largely almost inedible. The only respite in such a dreadful culinary régime was provided by tuck and by the fried doughnuts we were served once a week with a syrup sauce; there was little nutrition attached to these but their taste was delicious.

We each had a tuck tin that was kept locked in the cupboard in the Refectory and unlocked three times a day at break, after lunch and at tea. In the tuck tin we were allowed to keep sweets and cake, if our parents had sent us one. We used to secrete sweets in our knicker legs in order to smuggle them into the dormitory (out of bounds during the day) when no one was looking and place them under our pillows to eat in bed. Our special codeword for this was 'false teeth'!

My Aunt once sent me a chocolate cake and I felt I had rarely tasted anything so delicious. I managed to smuggle it out from beneath watchful eyes and shared it with two of the older girls who had a bedroom to themselves; they illicitly kept it for me there, a guilty secret. The arrival of parcels from home was eagerly looked forward to, but the gilt was removed from the gingerbread by the fact that we had to open them in Matron's presence and lock away the edible contents immediately in the tuck cupboard.

Nation-wide the stock response to any complaining was that there was a war on. In our case, however, wartime rationing could not be blamed entirely for the dreadful food we were served; for the most part bad cooking and the convent's need to economise were the main reasons. The first things that come to mind when former pupils meet and reminisce about schooldays are lumpy (and often burnt) porridge, pink semolina pudding and jugs of weak coffee with bits of skin floating on the top.

At breakfast we spooned up the thin gruel and left the huge lumps in our dishes. Eventually our form fared better; Shirley Harris was excused morning prayers in the chapel because she was Jewish, and therefore offered to begin dishing out the porridge. She made sure that the plates awaiting each of our form contained about a teaspoonful of gruel! Bacon, when we had it, consisted mostly of undercooked fat; fried eggs were usually overcooked, and the home-made bread was heavy and largely saltless; lumps of salt and of hardened flour appeared in it haphazardly. We were allowed a small square of margarine at teatime and an even smaller square of butter for breakfast; as this didn't stretch very far we tried to allay our hunger and conserve our marmite or jam by filling up with slices of dry bread upon which we scattered salt. For one whole term, I remember, soon after we had moved to Rise, the butter we were given was rancid.

Memories of lunchtime include stews containing lumps of gristly meat; slices of meat consisting mostly of fat; watery cabbage; whole boiled leeks; rice pudding with sultanas; pink lumpy semolina, or 'frogspawn'. Once a week we cheered loudly when the doughnuts appeared and we gobbled them up as quickly as possible in order to be first in the queue for seconds, the remaining doughnuts having been cut into halves to give more of us a fair share. Once a week, too, we were served either jam tart and custard, or pastry spread with a layer of jam and baked with the custard on top. These, unlike the milk puddings, were at least edible even if the pastry was a little hard.

Suppers, being meatless, were usually a little more palatable. Potatoes and onions cooked in milk were quite tasty and filling, as was macaroni cheese, but I dreaded the days when pilchards were served, because I just could not eat them and they ended up on somebody else's plate! The first course was usually followed by slab cake spread with jam, but when rhubarb was in season it was dished up to us day after day, stewed beyond recognition, stringy and sour, with a custard that was either too thin or too thick. Coffee again was served from large jugs. Just before bedtime jugs of steaming hot cocoa were wheeled into the hall on a trolley; at least we went to bed with a hot drink inside us.

A good half of the food we were given was thrown away and criminally wasted at a time when we were frequently reminded that children in Europe were starving. As we were required to leave clean plates, the inedible pieces of bacon or meat were either surreptitiously placed on a neighbour's plate when she wasn't looking or else passed down the line, under the table, until they reached the girl sitting nearest the open window; she would then toss it outside when Loffy was not looking. We were never discovered, either because a blind eye was turned or perhaps because Mother Hilda's dog, Molly, thinking that every other day was her birthday, consumed the evidence!

Unpalatable vegetables were harder to dispose of, and one of the few battles I have successfully waged with authority was over the leeks that Loffy once tried to force me to eat; after I had sat alone with her in the Refectory for half an hour after lunch, the leeks congealing on my plate, she finally conceded defeat. There was no escape, however, from pink semolina pudding, and our Convent upbringing led us cheerfully to make a joke of the concept of penitentially 'offering up' individual suffering in order to bring God's blessing on others. Before grimacing and downing each spoonful of pudding I, like the others, would for example say, 'One for mother; one for Dorothy; one for the starving children of Europe', and so on until the plate was finally clean.

Why did we not complain to our parents? For one thing, I don't think it occurred to most of us to do so and, even if it had, a deaf ear would probably have been turned: we had not been sent to boarding school for a life of luxury! I once complained to mother in the holidays about a punishment I had received and her only comment was that I must have deserved it; there was certainly no sympathy to be found in that direction. For another thing, we had to leave our letters home unsealed (ostensibly in case Mother Hilda wished to insert a communication to our parents) and we knew that she read them. In any case it was just another part of our being at boarding school and of what I have since realised was the nuns' life in miniature that we were expected to follow.

Life at Boynton was stark but we accepted it as our lot, although when speaking not so long ago to a fellow old pupil I did learn from her that she felt conditions had been too grim for an eight year old, the age at which she had first been sent away to school. We had no Common Room, only the main hall to play in. Free time was spent mostly, when not out of doors, in our classrooms; if we wished to sit and read a book we had to do so at our desks. Aunt Olive, who had disapproved strongly of my being sent away to school, especially a Catholic one ('they have to pay to go to Confession, you know') questioned me closely about conditions and was shocked to learn that there were no easy chairs, no home comforts of any kind. At the time her reaction surprised me: I had taken our lack of creature comforts for granted, having accepted them as being an inevitable part of school life, and I defended the nuns staunchly. No amount of physical discomfort could detract from the fact that I loved being at boarding school, and at least the deprivations made me appreciate my mother's home-cooking; it had the effect of making me far less faddy than I had been previously, a fact she was quick to note!

In spite of vicissitudes most of us were happy at Boynton. There were private miseries that I myself had to endure, but I did endure them and they did not prevent me from enjoying the manifold opportunities for fun and the companionship of girls of my own age. Life at Boynton, with its hardships counterbalanced by simplicity and innocence, truly reflected the meaning behind the emblem of the Order and its Founder: the Cross and the Lily.

Chapter Four

Although physically life was hard, the girls were friendly and I was immediately accepted, but Matron took an instant dislike to me. Shy and uncertain of myself, anxious to please, though not by any means an angel, and frequently misunderstood or my words misinterpreted, from the start I failed to make a good impression and many were the private miseries I suffered at her hands. Fortunately this was counter-balanced by the overall gentleness of the nuns.

The Religious Community at Boynton numbered ten: five black-veiled Choir nuns and five white-veiled Lay Sisters. Of the Choir nuns the two most dominant were Mère Marie de l'Enfant Jesus and Mother AElfreda.

Mother Hilda, who was in overall charge, was wise, kind, tolerant and indulgent. She always spoke quietly and never raised her voice in anger, but when she looked at us sternly from above her spectacles we knew we had overstepped the mark! Mother Aloysia (always known as Buggy because of her diminutive size) was kind but couldn't control us and, when roused, had a fearful temper which was fuelled from time to time by her pupils' ineptness. Mother Scholastica, whose English was poor, was fat and German (not a good thing to be during the war!) and we played her up. Mother Gertrud, who came over from Hull once a week and who, as a friend of my sister, had known me when I was a small child, was also German and we took advantage of her kind nature. We were, in fact, normal, naughty and spirited schoolgirls!

Mother AElfreda was lively and pretty, an excellent teacher and a good disciplinarian. She possessed a fertile brain, and her youthful enthusiasm and drive complemented Mother Hilda's greater wisdom and kindly approach.

Loffy was basically kind and affectionate, truly interested in and fond of us all; however, as she was in charge of us most of the time out of class and therefore handed out more Order Marks than the others, we failed to appreciate these aspects of her nature until we had left school. At one time our form became irritated when former pupils visited the school and remembered Loffy with affection; we signed a pact that when the time came for us to leave we would not follow suit. Naturally the pact was broken!

On the whole we were raised in an atmosphere of tolerance and broadmindedness. It was Matron and Miss Lee, not the nuns, who introduced the element of prudishness and narrow-mindedness normally associated with Convent Schools; fortunately it was not their influence, although it was damaging, but that of the nuns which formed our characters.

The attitude of those who are in charge of children can have an enormous effect for good or ill, as St Pierre Fourier, in his own gentleness and understanding, well knew. Matron's attitude verged at times on the cruel and I came to hate both her and her partner in crime. I was not alone in that, and they did quite a lot of harm in the school, but I was singled out and made a particular butt of their attention. I think this was because they could not believe that I was as naive as the impression I gave, although even Matron had to admit, when I eventually graduated to the small dormitory, that when she entered it to hand out Order Marks for talking I was usually fast asleep and not pretending to be.

Matron could not, in fact, accept that we were all naive. Many Convent schools have had a reputation for forbidding 'particular' friendships, and applied a rule that girls were not to go around together in two's. It was not an attitude adopted by our nuns and the word 'lesbianism' or even the thought of it was unknown to us.

Matron, however, introduced the concept of suspicion into the régime and made a great to-do one night after lights out when two of the girls were found in the same bed, reading a book together by the light of a torch. Reading with a torch under the bedclothes was a practice common to all of us who possessed one, and the two girls concerned had been totally innocent of anything untoward. We in fact knew very little about sex, and it was not until I was later about to leave school for University that Mother AElfreda, realising how incomplete my education was in this respect, gave me a book to read which explained the sexual act in mildly explicit terms. A former pupil remembers that when she left school at the age of sixteen she thought that babies came out of the mother's tummy. I am convinced that our lack of knowledge about sexual matters was a greater protection from harm than if we had been made fully aware of them; awareness leads to the desire for experimentation! Modern opinion will, of course, disagree!

Matron's usual weapon was the particularly nasty and deadly one of sarcasm, against which there is no possible comeback. One bedtime when, on passing her in the corridor, I politely said, 'Good evening, Matron,' her reply was, 'Butter wouldn't melt in your mouth, would it?' I had never heard the expression before and, taken aback, I asked the other girls what it meant. One of them explained, embarrassed at having to do so, and I was puzzled and hurt that simple politeness could have been so misinterpreted.

Eventually Matron's treatment of me became almost a joke, although psychologically it did considerable damage at a time when I needed to recover self-esteem. One evening, I remember, she poked her head round the partition when I was having a bath (the one time we could normally expect to have real privacy) and announced that she had reported me to Reverend Mother. I never did discover what I had done wrong!

Reverend Mother, who had remained at the Convent in Hull, was far too astute to take any notice, but the ears even of Mother Hilda, and especially Mother AElfreda, were certainly poisoned by the constant whisperings and pointed glances in my direction. Both Matrons had very dominant characters and excercised almost total influence over Mother AElfreda who was still young and not long out of the Noviciate. As she was extremely popular with most of us, her obvious dislike of me caused even more hidden suffering.

Mother AElfreda had been at school with my sister and that did not help matters; there was perhaps an assumption that I might be tempted to trade on the fact; certainly she was furious one day on finding a snapshot propped up on the classroom mantlepiece of Dorothy and herself when they were pupils at the Convent in Park Grove. Although I felt indignant when she furiously tore it up, especially as I had been urged by the others to display it, we accepted, at the time, that we had overstepped the mark. She had overreacted but in retrospect I can understand why.

Times have changed, but when we were at school there was great mystique attached to the nuns and a curiosity on our part as to what they looked like out of the habit. In the dormitory, we used to jump up and down on the bed next to Loffy's, trying to catch a glimpse of her over the curtain rail to see what she looked like without her veil! Now that the medieval habit has been abandoned and the mystique has disappeared along with it I am not sure that the change has been entirely for the better; some ineffable quality has been lost, an otherworldliness that made quite a deep impression on us spiritually when we were at school.

I myself was sensitive and vulnerable and had no weapons with which to counteract the kind of bullying I suffered at the hands of the Matrons, having never before encountered it. One incident of what amounted to cruelty, although certainly unrecognised as such by the perpetrator, caused me untold anguish. It happened one evening when Matron decided to do a neck inspection. Washing in a cold corridor in enamel basins that we had to fill with hot water and place on top of lockers (and in which we also had to clean our teeth) was not a task any of us relished; it was made worse by the fact that we were supposed to strip under our dressing-gowns and wash all over, a contortionist exercise that was extremely difficult. If we could get away with a lick and a promise we did so, but every now and then there were 'inspections'.

It was on one such occasion that I was found to have a tidemark round my neck. A scolding would have been fair enough, but the crime was treated as a matter almost worthy of expulsion! Matron hauled me downstairs, sat me on a chair in her sitting-room and summoned the nuns to witness my dirty neck. As I sat there scarlet-faced, they filed round me and pretended to be dutifully shocked. It was an incident totally out of keeping with the nuns' own style and indicative of how damaging an alien influence can be within a community noted for its kindness.

'Jinnie's dirty neck' was referred to by Matron on every possible occasion thereafter, seemingly as a joke, (although fortunately the nuns and the other girls did not share her warped sense of humour) and my loathing of the woman responsible was increased even further; I had been made to suffer a public disgrace out of all proportion to the crime and my fragile self-esteem had been lowered even further.

Our gentle Founder would not have approved! He had once written to one of his Convents where the discipline, after a change of Superior, had become too harsh: 'I should advise your trying to placate or appease the two poor girls who recently had the cane for I don't know what little squabbles, and show them and their companions, by word and deed, that you intend to treat them more gently, and every day give them a few cherries, which are not dear, or some other titbit, for their tea...'

I had already, however, become used to adversity, and the fact that the private purgatory I suffered did not detract from my overall happiness at school was due in large measure to the generally relaxed atmosphere at Boynton, to the freedom we were allowed and to the fact that I related well with my classmates and to the nuns in general. Only recently a contemporary of mine, whom I had not seen since she left school, said to me, 'Do you remember that dreadful Matron we had? I hated her!' It was comforting to be reassured that I was not the only one who had suffered.

Although I hated the Matrons I continued to hope for Mother AElfreda's favour despite her poor opinion of me. Once a week it was her task to drive the school's ancient Wolsley into Hull in order to take the laundry to the Convent there. As the Bishop had ruled (following Mother Dorothea's escapades) that she was to be accompanied by another person, members of my form were given that privilege in turn. It meant an escape from school, a few hours at home for those who lived in Hull, and a drive there and back in Mother AElfreda's company, and the outing was eagerly looked forward to. I found, not surprisingly, that I was left to the last!

When my turn could not be escaped, it was obvious that Mother AElfreda was not looking forward to having to take me. Conversation during the drive was rather laboured, as I was shy and tongue-tied, but I remember telling her that my favourite subject was English (which, along with Geography and History, was taught by her.) She seemed surprised, especially when I told her I had always come top in that subject at my previous school; in her lessons I had been receiving low marks. She appeared to regard me with new interest and when, the following year, I won a national essay competition, my academic ability became gradually recognised and encouraged. Mother AElfreda and I eventually became close friends both before and after I left school, but not until the departure of the Matrons, whose harmful effect was finally recognised as being contradictory to the Spirit of the Order and its Founders.

Chapter Five

When I first went to Boynton Hall, there were only about thirty-six pupils, all boarders apart from one or two local girls; we all came from the East Riding, many of us from Hull where the French Convent had long had an excellent reputation.

Because numbers were so few, the classes were necessarily of mixed ability but at least we had the benefit of individual attention. Having arrived with good reports from my previous school, I was placed in a form with children older than myself, some of them two or three years older.

I can picture our form-room to this day, with its sturdy wooden desks and the initials of generations of pupils carved into the lids; it was on the second floor of the building overlooking the drive. An old-fashioned blackboard and easel stood by the sash window and a log fire burned in the grate. I can picture the other girls who occupied the desks: Rosemary Brocklehurst, Shirley Harris, June Tong, Margaret Amos, Mary Giblin, Joanna Scanlan and, later, Maureen Matthews. Of mixed ability, individual personalities and of varying shapes and sizes, we lived, worked and played together and, with the exception of one girl, had a good time.

On re-reading my school reports from Boynton not long ago I was a little surprised to notice that for the first two years my position in most subjects except French was usually near the bottom of the class and my marks were poor. I consistently received a 'Very Good' for needlework and Art, although I had little aptitude for either subject, and those overgenerous remarks must be attributed to the respective kindness of Mother Gertrud and Buggy. Not even the latter, however, was able to summon up more than a few per cent for my marks in Mathematics.

The fact that I seemed not to shine academically was probably because I was working with girls one or two years my senior. I enjoyed most of the lessons, but academic prowess was not at that time considered to be of prime importance in the environment into which I had been propelled. My mother later confessed that a good academic education had not been uppermost in her mind when sending me to Boynton; she had wanted me to acquire the finish and values the French Convent was well known for. We were certainly given a good grounding in manners, courtesy and consideration for others; we were also encouraged to think and act independently and learnt to be broadminded.

No one could say that at Boynton we were under pressure. Life was relaxed and rules were kept to a minimum. There was discipline, irksome restrictions with regard to talking, together with physical hardships, but on the whole we were made to conform only to standards of decency, politeness and courtesy. Although we were at school to be taught, actual lessons were only a part of our education and if they were cancelled it was not in those early days felt that our parents were being cheated. Somehow the holiday atmosphere of Boynton as it was before the war had been retained.

Lessons were indeed cancelled frequently and for various reasons. Apart from Matron, Miss Lee and Miss Hay who came from Scarborough once a week to teach ballet there were no lay members of staff; the few nuns who were there had to share the teaching between them. If one of them were absent we joyfully received the news that we would have a free period. Often it meant several free periods because Mother AElfreda and Buggy between them had to teach several different subjects. If either of them were ill, Loffy or Mother Scholastica sat with us for a study period. If no one was available to supervise we were sometimes sent outside to play our favourite game of 'Reserve', otherwise we were put 'on our honour' to behave.

Our honour did not extend to neglecting an opportunity for fun, usually at Mother Scholastica's expense. Many Boynton Girls will remember the occasion one morning when our form was on its honour in the classroom immediately above that in which she was teaching. Shirley Harris happened to have her red dressing-gown in the classroom and we dangled this through the open sash window on a piece of string. The children in the room below were astonished and amused at its sudden appearance. It dangled for a few seconds and then was withdrawn and the process was repeated. Finally, her lesson having been constantly interrupted by laughter, Scholly caught a glimpse of the cause of it, downed tools and laboured up the stairs to our classroom. Having been warned by bush telegraph of her coming, we were found to all intents and purposes with our noses deep in our books. She gave us a stern warning, threatened us with Order Marks and departed.

Five minutes later Mother Scholastica was back again, the warning having been ignored. Reluctant to carry out her threat, she gave us a further warning which again went unheeded. Highly delighted at the welcome diversion, her pupils dissolved into uncontrollable laughter when they saw the dressing-gown descend yet again. Once more poor Scholly laboured up the stairs: 'You know what you 'ave,' she said to us sternly. With our usual casuistry, we did not feel morally obliged to report the Order Marks, as she had not actually been specific.

If we had dared to play such a trick on Mother AElfreda she would have punished us swiftly, but children are quick to seize a chink in another's armour. We were not aware that Mother Scholastica had an illness, nor did it occur to us that she must have been feeling very alienated; she had in fact been interned on the Isle of Man during the first part of the war. We went through a silly period, I remember, of pretending that she was a German spy, although we kept our imaginative playacting to ourselves and it was a childish game that she was unaware of.

Although we were never rude to her, Mother Scholastica was our least favourite nun; she was very Teutonic, rather aloof and did not understand English ways. Detailed one day to take us out for a walk, she reported us to Mother Hilda because we had picked some of the wild strawberries in a wood; she told us that German children wouldn't dream of doing such a thing! Mother Hilda, as English as the other was German, privately told us not to let her see us pick them the next time! When the war ended Mother Scholastica returned to Germany, no doubt thankful to be back among children who were better behaved than we were.

Chapter Six

One winter term nearly the whole school fell victim to a severe epidemic of 'flu. Classes had to be abandoned, and when the sickbay was full the small dormitory was turned into a sickroom and some of the nuns had to help with the nursing.

Those children who were still on their feet were sent for long walks in the crisp air: those who were ill were cosseted and tended with care; it was not long before I joined their ranks. The doctor came daily but could do little except advise that we be kept warm. Fires were kept alight in the sickrooms and it was a lovely sensation to fall asleep to the flickering of the flames, the cracking of twigs and the falling of logs. Before the lights were turned out we were given drinks of hot milk containing a spoonful of golden syrup, and at intervals throughout the day we sat up in bed, with a towel over our heads and holding an enamel bowl from which to inhale.

Matron's passion for fresh air, and the rigorous conditions under which we normally slept, had not been able to prevent the epidemic. Nevertheless the belief in healthy exercise and fresh air was maintained. Along one of the lanes in the park in front of the Hall grew masses of snowdrops which the Convent sold to a shop in Bridlington. At snowdrop time we would frequently be told that it as it was such a clear, fresh day a walk would do us good; lessons were cancelled for the morning and we were sent to pick snowdrops. Naturally we made no objection, nor did we object when afternoon lessons were abandoned in order to allow us to go sledging at 'Little Switzerland' or to have an interhouse snowball match.

The winters were particularly severe in those days, with heavy falls of snow. The fun of tobogganing was enhanced one afternoon when we persuaded Loffy to take a turn on a sledge. She was given a push and, with veil flying, arms flailing and white-stockinged legs exposed, she descended the slope at top speed and fell off halfway down, hurting her leg. For a while after that she walked with a limp but lost our sympathy when we noticed that the limp became obvious only when she saw us in the vicinity.

Botany lessons with Mother Aloysia frequently took the form of 'wooding' in winter and nature walks in the garden in summer. They were a welcome diversion from having to learn endless lists of species, their genus and Latin names. Buggy, although then the only one of the nuns at Boynton to possess a degree, was not a good teacher and, in some of the subjects for which she was detailed to take us, it was a question of having to keep one step ahead of us; this meant almost solely textbook teaching, and we found the lessons very boring.

I remember nothing about Botany except the words 'stamen' and 'photosynthesis', but I do remember strolls in summer by the flowerbeds during which Buggy attempted to give us some practical teaching especially the time when someone gave her a little push as she was bending over to show us a flower and she fell into the middle of a clump of blooms. It was fortunate that she didn't have far to fall, being so tiny! Convent schoolgirls can be as thoughtlessly cruel as any others. There was no malice towards Buggy; it was just silly, childish fun and on that occasion she had the good sense to take it in that spirit. At least she did not have to contend with impoliteness, which sadly is so often the lot of teachers nowadays.

Buggy had to take us for Art, Latin, Botany, Maths, Scripture and Singing and her teaching life must have been purgatory for her. Margaret Amos, the only one of us who possessed natural mathematical ability, unwittingly one lesson exposed poor Mother Aloysia's ignorance of the term 'pi'. The rest of us had never heard of it, but unfortunately for Buggy Margaret's father was an excellent mathematician and she must have learnt it from him.

We did, in fact, feel sorry for Mother Aloysia, knowing her intellectual brilliance and recognising that, in having to teach subjects that were not her own to children whose interest she could not arouse, she was unhappy and out of her depth. Because she took upon herself the most menial tasks, we regarded her as a saint, but that didn't prevent us from taking advantage. Perhaps, in writing an account of our schooldays, it would have been more politic not to portray our own definite lack of sanctity, but we were trained to be forthright and honest!

When Buggy wasn't washing up piles of dirty dishes and pans, she could be seen in the garden or around the perimeter with a wheelbarrow collecting twigs, for she was the one who lit all the fires in the Hall each day. When Botany lessons were replaced by excursions up the 'Valley' to collect wood, we co-operated willingly. Latin lessons could not be escaped so easily but we learnt very little, for each one of us had a favourite book open on our knees under cover of our desks. When reminiscing with a friend about those lessons, we both recalled that one of the few bits of Latin we could remember from Mother Aloysia's lessons was the irregular imperatives for which, with a flash of brilliance, she had devised the sentence, 'Dic had a duc with fur on and that's a fac.'

Mother Aloysia tried hard to make her lessons more interesting. She had a little stock of jokes. One of them was of a boy at boarding school who sent a postcard to his father saying only, 'No mun, no fun, your son.' The reply he received was equally succinct: 'How sad! Too bad! Your dad.' Another one at least succeeded in teaching us the endings of the First Conjugation. It was about a boy who was not paying attention in class; when the master told him to conjugate a certain verb, the offender asked his neighbour sotto voce what verb the master had told him to conjugate. 'Damned if I know!' replied his neighbour, whereupon the offender stood up and recited,

'damnedifino!
damnedifinas!
damnedifinat!
damnedifinamus!
damnedifinatis!
damnedifinant!

Unfortunately such inspirational teaching on Buggy's part was only rare and we quickly returned to reading our novels surreptitiously, with the result that when examination time came we always failed abysmally. Taking this as personal failure, Buggy one time lost her temper, throwing our papers at us and making us resit the exam. This left us temporarily chastened but unrepentant.

On one occasion, after we had moved from Boynton, our classroom conveniently being on the ground floor, we disappeared one by one through the open window and hid in the garden. On finally looking up from the Caesar she had been translating for us, Buggy found that the classroom was bare!

It is easy in retrospect to be ashamed of our behaviour, but children are not naturally thoughtful when it is a matter of playing on the weakness of their teachers, and we were no exception. Mother Aloysia was forgiving and kind, and made the mistake of rarely punishing us; she was also, I am sure, painfully aware of her inability to hold our attention and maintain discipline.

Loffy, on the other hand, was an excellent teacher and gave us a thorough grounding in French. She also made a habit of speaking to us in her native language and of conducting prayers in it, and we left school with an excellent accent and a superior understanding of spoken French. Her attempts to persuade us to speak in that language during mealtimes and on walks, however, met with less success.

Mother AElfreda took us for English, History, Geography and, later, Scripture; no doubt Mother Aloysia had finally rebelled against having to teach a subject that laid her open to having to parry our seemingly innocent questions of 'What is adultery, Mother?' or 'What is a decreenisi?' Mother AElfreda, though unqualified at that time (she took a BA Hons degree in English several years later) was a born teacher; we enjoyed her lessons, and her own love of English caused most of us to love and appreciate it too. Although Study periods were usually spent having to learn poetry or long speeches from Shakespeare, it was a chore for which I have ever since been grateful and I think none of us found Shakespeare boring.

We did not like having to miss Mother AElfreda's lessons; we learnt a great deal in them and there was never any attempt to play her up. She did, unfortunately, suffer very badly from migraines and her lessons were often cancelled. We could sympathise with her migraines but were less tolerant of the frequent interruptions caused by Matron. When the door of the classroom opened and her head appeared round it with the summons, 'Can I have a word, Mother AElfreda?' we inwardly groaned and resigned ourselves to twenty or thirty wasted minutes of precious lesson time.

Reverend Mother frequently telephoned Mother AElfreda from Hull and would usually talk to her for at least an hour. When School Certificate approached, these interruptions nearly drove us frantic.

Mother AElfreda also took us for Elocution and Drama and many were the scenes from Shakespeare that we performed for the whole school. No Boynton girl will ever forget Shirley Harris in the role of Shylock; she was a natural actress but also, being Jewish, she put her heart and soul into the part. No one begrudged June Tong the role of Portia.

I was always given a male role to play, being thin, gawky and not pretty; I was familiarly known as 'skinny Jinny' whereas my friend, Maureen Matthews, was known as 'fatty Matty'. My own hour of triumph eventually came several years later, however, when I played Bottom in an end-of-term production of 'A Midsummer Night's Dream'. Amazingly, the performance I gave received great acclaim and thus boosted my self-confidence.

The casual approach to our academic education at Boynton would cause hands to be raised in horror nowadays. Suffice it to say that of the pupils there Shirley Harris and I both went to University and obtained degrees, Maureen Matthews became a physiotherapist, and others have distinguished themselves in various ways and in many different professions. There were gaps in my own education, particularly in the scientific field, but as I have not been endowed with a scientific brain I have never felt that mattered very much. More important is the fact that when we meet together as former pupils we still like one another, can relate instantly together, have retained the values that were absorbed at school and have extremely fond memories of our schooldays along with affection for, and loyalty towards, the Convent. We were surely very well educated!

As I grew in years I gradually matured academically and eventually became top of the class. This was no big deal in a small school but, more importantly, I had learnt how to study, to think for myself and to apply myself. We all learnt to be interested in life and culture, and to be able to get along well with our contemporaries as well as with most older and younger people.

On the other hand, the damage done by the Matrons at Boynton left a permanent mark on me at least, and I personally have never succeeded in coping with hostility. The education we received, the politeness that was instilled in us, and the atmosphere in which we grew up did not in fact prepare us for that, and perhaps in this respect it could be argued that we were disadvantaged! I feel sure, however, that a training in courtesy is preferable to a grounding in rudeness.

Chapter Seven

Life was by no stretch of the imagination all work and no play, and Boynton Hall was a paradise for imaginative and romantically minded children - apart from the cold. Young as we were, we appreciated the historical significance of the Elizabethan mansion.

In the village church at the top of the drive the lectern is in the form of a turkey, for it was William Strickland, a navigator, who had first introduced turkeys to England. Hanging in our Refectory was a portrait of Queen Henrietta Maria, wife of King Charles 1st; she had sent it in recompense for having taken the family plate when she was penniless and in flight from the Roundheads. The Queen had hidden in the grounds, under the bridge over the Gypsy Race, and the Strickland family had taken pity on her, although at that period Parliamentarians under Cromwell.

In the Big Dormitory a part of the bookshelves could be pushed back to reveal a Priest's Hole, and at the far end also of what had formerly been the library there was a large walk-in cupboard leading from which was a secret passage. Such relics from the past were exciting and entry was never forbidden, but both the hole and the passage smelt damp and musty and we were not tempted to remain in them for long.

On rainy days, after our formroom had been transferred to the Book-Room which led from the former library, we would sometimes take down the large volume of Fox's Martyrs from one of the shelves. Fascinated and horrified by the gruesome drawings, we learnt more about suffering for the Faith than anything that could have been taught us by word of mouth. Offering up lumpy semolina was infinitely preferable to being hanged, drawn and quartered, and unlike T.S.Eliot's Thomas à Becket I for one had no untoward desire for a martyr's crown, much as I revered those who had died so horribly for their beliefs.

Beneath the wooden staircase by the library there was said to be a skull that shrieked. We never heard it, but Mother Dorothea was reputed to have done so. Former pupils will be disappointed to hear that the present owner of the Hall has dismissed the rumour as being apocryphal.

No one in our time reportedly had ever witnessed the ghost of wicked Sir Walter Strickland, hanged for the murder of his brother. His life-size portrait hung in the Music Room and eyed us malevolently during music lessons or choir practice. The portrait had been painted in such a way that his eyes really did seem to follow us.

In the main hall, which had four thick stone pillars, there were tapestries on the walls and near these were pedestals holding stone busts; we treated the latter irreverently, using them to serve as goal-posts when we kicked a netball around. They and the tapestries frequently received the full force of that same netball in our many games of Reserve. Fortunately we did no damage, for it was discovered afterwards that they were quite valuable!

There were two beautiful lawns, the South Lawn and the West Lawn; there was a Lovers' Walk, a Folly and a large kitchen garden. One side of the drive was partly wooded and provided a golden opportunity for the forbidden pastime of tree-climbing. I once fell out of a tree into a bed of nettles and had to go to Benediction straight afterwards in considerable agony from the stings I had received; it was a just penance for disobedience.

The long Gallery which housed the chapel was a beautiful room, as was the oak-panelled Music Room, entrance hall and stairway by the West Porch. Behind one of the panels on the staircase were the remains of a doorway, relic of the site upon which a medieval house had formerly stood, although at the time we were unaware of this.

It was as well that we were able to glory in the past history of the Hall, for its twentieth century realities were far from romantic except when the electrical circuit broke down and, plunged into blackness, we had to walk around with lighted candles.

There were no washbasins, only the occasional sink, and as there were few lavatories available to us, it was as well that we were few in number. Such as they were, they provided us with snippets of news from the outside world. In wartime, paper was precious and toilet rolls were replaced by squares of newspaper hanging by a string. As we had no other access to newspapers, this made it tempting to linger longer than was necessary but was also frustrating, for it was necessary to try to piece them together in order to make sense of the words printed there.

Of periodical embarrassing torture for girls was the absence of an incinerator or even sanitory bins. Instead of the latter there was a long, wooden contraption behind the door at the far end of the corridor where we had to wash. In the days when unmentionables were unmentionable, we carried the former in our knicker-legs or dressing-gown pockets, until the way was clear for us to go to the disposal unit when no one was about.

However, the archaic conditions and the hardships of life at Boynton were more than compensated for by our close relationship with history and with nature, and by the tremendous amount of fun we had. Many memories abound.

On winter evenings in our last year at Boynton members of our form were allowed to use Mother Hilda's sitting-room for the hour between supper and bedtime, and we relished the privilege. It was a small, cosy room with chintz-covered armchairs, and we felt at home clustered round the electric fire, playing old, scratched records on an ancient portable gramophone. I remember endless games of 'Truth or Dare' as we sat in the darkness with the lights switched off and with only the glow of the fire. I believe we also used to toast bread there but my memory is hazy; we certainly did so at the fire in our formroom.

It was in Mother Hilda's office, situated next to her sitting-room, that the seniors gathered to listen to the historic D Day broadcast, for we ourselves had no wireless. Although generally we felt far removed from the war, we were always aware of it and longed for it to end. It was at her office, too, that we all had to line up on winter mornings to receive a spoonful of Cod Liver Oil and Malt. Molly, Mother Hilda's spaniel, used to join the queue for her daily dose.

The boisterous game of Reserve that we played in the stone-flagged main hall in winter had been imported by Mother Gertrud from Germany. I have come across no-one else in England who has heard of it. Reserve was a marvellous game. Two girls picked teams, those who were chosen first being the ones who could throw a netball the hardest and be able to catch it without letting it drop. Shirley Harris was the best player in that respect.

The teams faced each other, divided by a line drawn by placing our sashes along the ground, with a 'reserve' from the other side placed behind each team. The object of the game was to throw the ball as hard as possible against someone on the opposite side, the opponents trying to dodge it; if the ball missed, someone in the other team caught it and threw it over to the reserve or else aimed from behind at the opposing team. If the ball touched someone, or was caught but dropped, that person was 'out' and helped the reserve behind the line by running for the ball, and the game continued until all the players in one of the teams had been eliminated. In summer we played Reserve outside, and when she was free Mother AElfreda took little persuasion to join in.

Another game we played outside was 'Kick Ball and Fly'. The one chosen to be 'it' had to kick the netball as far as she could, call out the name of one of the others and then run away with the rest to hide; the person whose name had been called had to retrieve the ball, count up to a hundred and then go in search of the others. I think the first one to be found had to kick the ball the next time, the rest having come out of hiding.

'Eggy' was also popular. As far as I can remember, the one who was 'it' had to throw a tennis ball into the air whilst the others ran away; she then called out the name of one of them before she too ran off. When that person had caught or retrieved the ball she shouted 'Eggy!' (which meant 'egg, if you budge') and the rest had to 'freeze'. She then did a hop, skip, jump and a spit towards the nearest one and attempt to hit her by throwing the ball. I think the game ended by the players forming a long arch against a wall, through which the girl who was hit had to run the gauntlet.

Our games were noisy and hilarious and the nuns accepted this indulgently; occasionally pent-up energy would erupt into what Mother Hilda called our 'mad half-hour'. One such occasion brought down on our heads the wrath of Father Reilly, the Chaplain. He was a sick man, suffering from diabetes and consequently short-tempered, and his sitting-room was directly above our formroom. One Sunday afternoon during a particularly rowdy half-hour the door was flung open and an irate voice bellowed, 'It's like a bear-garden in here!' Immediately subdued, for we were rather afraid of him, we slunk out tail between legs. Although he reported us to

Mother Hilda, she took no action, only teasing us afterwards by referring to our formroom as 'the Bear Garden' and calling us 'the Bears'. We did try to be more considerate in future, although I am not sure whether it was before or after that episode that one of the girls accidentally sent a cricket ball through his window.

The Catholics especially had a trying time with Father Reilly because he was apparently not the gentlest of confessors. 'Midnight' feasts had to begin and end before midnight, otherwise the Catholics would have to confess to having broken the fast, which in those days lasted from midnight until after Mass.

The Chaplain did occasionally show another side to his nature, though, and one day, when we were on the lawn practising for a Gym Display, he came out and couldn't resist a boyish inclination to jump over the 'horse'. We watched in amazement, fearful for him because of his bad state of health but warming to him nevertheless. Not many months later, after the move to Rise, he died.

No Boynton girl will ever forget Mother AElfreda's Greek Dancing phase. We were sent home at the end of one term with a letter to our parents requesting them to buy silky black-out material and make it up into tunics according to the pattern in an accompanying sketch. The next term, on a Sunday evening after supper, lessons began. We were not very enthusiastic and regarded it all as a joke.

Having placed us at the four pillars in the hall, Mother AElfreda stood in the middle, skirts tucked through her pockets, sleeves rolled up and an open instruction booklet in her hand. Assuming the required positions, we each in turn glided as gracefully as possible to the pillar diagonally opposite the one by which we had been standing. This caused much hilarity. Because our heads were lowered according to the posture demanded, there was a great deal of bumping into one another as we followed the instruction to cross the hall diagonally and simultaneously. The good-humoured laughter increased when we were told to stand at ease and watch whilst Mother AElfreda gave us a demonstration.

The Greek Dancing phase was short-lived; either Mother AElfreda lost interest or our lack of enthusiasm made itself palpably felt. With relief we returned to the more enjoyable exercise of English Country Dancing. This was organised by Mother AElfreda, with Buggy at the piano, and we danced our way merrily through 'Strip the Willow', the Eightsome Reel and 'Sir Roger de Coverley'.

P.T. lessons, also taken by Mother AElfreda, provided much laughter. We had no gymnasium, nor at first was there any equipment until a horse was transported from the Hull Convent; previous to that the only 'horse' we had was an upturned fireguard. The lessons were fraught with danger, but those were the days before people thought of suing for damages or of the need to be insured against eventualities. Later, when teaching at a state school, I was amazed and frustrated by the restrictions placed on the teachers because of the fear of lawsuits. I am quite sure that if one of us at Boynton had come to grief over the fireguard the parents concerned would not have thought of taking any action; accidents were seen as just one of the normal hazards of life, whether at home or at school. Fortunately no-one did come to any harm during those lessons.

Chapter Eight

The South Lawn was of the right size for playing hockey, which I enjoyed once I had rebelled against always having to play goalie. On my arrival at Boynton I had been flattered into taking that unpopupar position, assured by Mother AElfreda and the girls that I was the best goalie they had. After a couple of terms of standing half-frozen between the goalposts, I announced that I would like to try playing centre-half instead. It was discovered that I could run fast and I kept that position until I was promoted to centre-forward. There proved to be some things I was able to shine at and I became the school's fastest runner and highest jumper. I was also the best piano player! There was a distinct advantage in attending a small school and being a large fish in a small pool: I didn't have much competition.

Poor little Buggy's purgatory was increased by having to give piano lessons, for which our parents paid extra. I was her star pupil, the only one who made her life worthwhile. I hope that when Judgement Day comes, that will be weighed against all the times I helped to make her life a misery. I happened to be the only one of Mother Aloysia's pupils to possess any musical talent, although I never took an examination and my knowledge of theory was elementary. Her other pupils learnt under sufferance and were the cause to her of many a self-imposed penance. Regularly, on crossing through the hall where she was giving a piano lesson, we found her banging the fingers of her unfortunate pupils hard down on the keys in frustration and temper.

Singing lessons were also under Buggy's tutelage and must have been a cause of dread to her; we used to play her up unmercifully. Tired of singing 'Will ye no come back again?' from the Community Song Book, we usually ended by standing on our benches in the hall, crawling underneath them and generally committing mayhem. A few years later, when a Singing Mistress came out to Rise from Hull once a week, what a difference it made! She was qualified, experienced, had a lovely voice and we sang beautiful songs in harmony; we loved her lessons.

Between tea and supper there were two hours of silent Study, supervised by Loffy in the Study Hall; it was during that time that some of our piano practices were scheduled. When I was practising in the room below, the other girls used to excuse themselves one by one and come to the piano to listen. It was not that they marvelled at my technique (which was decidedly shaky) but because I soon tired of practising my set pieces and would play ones that I liked and which I had borrowed from mother's music cabinet at home.

'The Isle of Capri', 'Underneath the Spreading Chestnut Tree', 'Ramona', 'Sonny Boy', 'Deep Purple' all eventually attracted an audience until Loffy sent a messenger down to see what had become of them. 'The Moonlight Sonata' also was a favourite, along with 'The Rustle of Spring' and 'Claire de Lune'. My proficiency in the first did not extend far beyond the first movement, but that was of no consequence for by then the others were in danger of collecting one of Loffy's Order Marks!

It was during one of my music lessons that Mother Aloysia put me on the spot by asking me to tell her the nickname she had been given. Mère Marie de l'Enfant Jesus had complained to the Community that it was disrespectful for the girls to refer to her as 'Loffy', and Mother Aloysia was innocently curious as to what we called her. Encouraged to speak honestly, I felt this was not an occasion when it would be politic to do so, for although we took advantage of her lack of discipline we were fond of her and in no way could I deliberately hurt her feelings. On seeing my hesitation,

Buggy herself suggested that perhaps she was called 'Alo', the affectionate name she said she was given by the nuns, and I gratefully said, 'Yes, Mother', feeling that a white lie was justified on that occasion.

We loved it when Father Redmund, the Parish Priest of St Vincent's in Hull, came to visit us. He used to turn up uninvited and unannounced, hat on the back of his head, cigarette dangling from his lips, and we would rush to greet him. School routine was disrupted as we entreated him to play the piano for us, and he would sit down and play Chopin's Funeral March and the Revolutionary Polonaise, finishing with 'My Grandfather's Clock'. During the latter he tapped on the frame of the piano at the appropriate times and we loved it. He in turn adored the adulation he received though I gather his parishioners suffered from his constant absences. Following his visits we used to find a cake on one of our beds, labelled 'For a Midnight Feast', and we took full advantage of that, the nuns obligingly turning a blind eye. Mother Hilda did, however, remind us in Assembly one day that one of the stair-treads creaked!

Occasionally Father Redmund was commandeered to conduct Benediction if Father Reilly was unwell. We liked this, because he used to go through the Rosary at lightning speed, and he was so absentminded he frequently approached the altar in his carpet slippers, causing suppressed giggles from among the rows of white-veiled children. Always intent on getting through the Rosary as quickly as possible, we took our cue from him which landed us in trouble when Father Reilly made his reappearance. After we had gabbled our way through the First Mystery, he turned round one evening and said sternly, 'We are not sending telegrams to Heaven.'

There was great excitement one morning when one of the younger children reported having had a vision of an angel on the

South Lawn the previous night. She was so convincing, everyone began to wonder whether we had a saint in our midst and whether it should be reported to the Bishop. Sanity prevailed, and the 'vision' was put down to a bout of religious fervour and a fevered imagination, probably induced by the film of 'The Song of Bernadette' we had been shown.

At one time some of us were intrigued by the Stigmata and used to examine our hands at intervals to see if the marks of Christ's nails had appeared there! On the whole we were healthily irreligious but innately spiritual and firm in our faith in God. From time to time we unselfconsciously and individually popped into chapel to say a prayer for a special intention. (Usually it was something like, 'Dear God, please let it be fine for Sports Day'!)

Reverend Mother's feast-day called for 'spiritual bouquets'. This meant that we each gabbled 'Our Father', 'Hail Mary' and 'Glory Be' as many times as we could, reported the final number to our House Captains and had the satisfaction of knowing that on the back of the Holy Picture sent to Reverend Mother our prayers for her would be recorded: two thousand Our Fathers, five thousand Hail Marys etcetera. I am sure she was not deceived as to the lack of true fervour with which the prayers had been said.

Chapter Nine

We were very innocent, unsophisticated and school-girlish in the fun we derived and devised, and this was highlighted one day by the arrival in midterm of a new girl. Legend had preceded her, for we heard that she had been expelled from St Mary's in Hull. Oh, là, là! We decided that she probably needed taking down a peg or two. As it happened, she was more than a match for us.

Before Barbara arrived we had decided to introduce ourselves by false and ridiculous names. She took the wind out of our sails by striding into the dormitory, holding out her hand in greeting and saying confidently, 'Hello! I'm Barbara Buchanan. What are your names?'

Awestruck by her sophistication and self-confidence, we were soon eating out of her hand and eagerly enquired what dreadful crime she had committed to have been expelled from school. Compared with us she was a woman of the world and the fact that her father was a bookmaker added height to her growing dimension.

Barbara became popular among us but never quite fitted into boarding school life, and on V.E. Day she caused a stir by running away, as she wanted to be in on the fun in Hull. Her father brought her back the next day and she remained for the rest of her School Certificate year, after which she thankfully left school. We kept in touch with her, seeing her in the holidays and receiving letters and occasional visits at weekends. Not long after this we were shattered to learn that she had developed leukaemia. Previously so full of life, she died at the age of twenty-one.

One morning Mother Hilda received a visit from the irate mother of one of the village boys. The previous evening two ghostly figures clad in white sheets had appeared in the drive, outside our formroom. Shirley Harris had thrown a bottle of ink at them and they had turned tail and fled. The mother of the one whom the ink had hit complained of the damage done to her sheet, but I believe received little sympathy from Mother Hilda.

We were not closed in by walls and gates; local crime was virtually unknown and the villagers did not normally trespass. We had a great deal of freedom within the limited amount of time we had to ourselves, and were readily given permission to walk down the village or go for bicycle rides; we were in the country and little harm could befall us. Where bounds are not set there is little need to rebel in that area. That did not, however, prevent fertile minds from thinking up means to add extra fun and excitement to our lives.

Ghosts and spooks were in the air after the ink-bottle episode and one day, instigated by Joanna Scanlan, we thought up a daring plan: we would slip out of the building after dark, go to the churchyard beyond the entrance to the drive and have a midnight feast there. Not quite brave enough to go at midnight, we went at eight o'clock in the evening, when we thought Matron and the nuns would be occupied with their own activities.

The night was dark and the graveyard was eerie but we bravely went through with our venture, sitting on Sir William Strickland's grave and eating oranges. When we returned to school, giggling and pleased with ourselves, we were greeted by Matron, who had found Shirley alone in the formroom (for as Head-Girl she had felt in conscience bound to opt out of the escapade) and had made her disclose our whereabouts. What a commotion there was! Lacking as always a sense of proportion, Matron saw our misdemeanour in the light of a major crime and Mother Hilda felt in duty bound to support her.

We had expected to be punished if found out, for there would have been no excitement otherwise, but the disgrace we were made to undergo was, we felt, excessive! As we were then Games and House Captains and had, we were told, betrayed our positions of trust and responsibility, it was decided that we should suffer the disgrace of being given four Order Marks each (two was usually the maximum at one go) which then had to be read out in Assembly and our crime confessed to in front of the lesser mortals over whom we normally held sway. On top of that we were sent to bed the next evening at six-thirty with the 'babies', after having first, in silence, shared their supper of bread and milk.

The youngest children were curious but bemused, and the rest of the school thought it hugely amusing and were envious of the initiative we had shown. The nuns tried to be solemn but joked and teased us about it ever after. It was, however, another example of Matron's propensity to inflict humiliation which, like sarcasm, is a psychologically harmful and dangerous weapon.

In terms of crime and punishment it is interesting to compare those days, back in the 1940's, with today's climate. We were normal, mischievous schoolgirls but were not rude, cheeky or openly defiant. Today it would be virtually impossible to control behaviour almost solely by the handing out of Order Marks with some form of minor detention for those who collected too many.

The graveyard episode, at an era when we had been most unlikely to have come to harm, was magnified out of all proportion, and represented the height of delinquency of fourteen and fifteen year olds at our school. More shocking perhaps, in the eyes of some, might have been the craze we developed for playing Pontoon with the Black Baby money that was in our care! We paid it back, of course, and I am quite sure the nuns knew what we were doing but

Mother Hilda, had she caught us, would not have had the proverbial leg to stand on. She herself once handed the Black Baby money to Maureen Matthews (whose father was an avid race-goer when he wasn't being an army officer) to put on a horse during the holidays. The horse as it happened won, and doubled the amount of money to be sent to the African Missions, but Maureen said that if it hadn't won her father would have felt obliged to pretend that it had!

We were allowed to have bicycles at school and to go for rides at the weekends when we were older. One warm summer's day a friend and I asked permission to go for a ride but didn't specify our destination, intending to have an 'illicit' afternoon on the beach at Carnaby, several miles away. On the return journey I went too fast round a bend and came off my bicycle, deeply gashing a knee. For once I received some sympathy, this time undeserved, from Matron who had to deal with the wound. It should have been stitched, but after what seemed a very long time it eventually healed, leaving a reminder of my misdemeanour in the form of a permanent scar. We felt we had been very daring to break bounds that had not actually been specified, but we would have received permission to go to Carnaby had we sought it; it was just another example of young people naturally craving adventure and of creating for themselves some excitement in a régime that was not too strict or restrictive.

The fact that we were so happy at Boynton was due in no small measure to the wisdom of Mother Hilda, to her tolerance and broad-minded approach and to an absence of undue pressure. The nuns were truly in loco parentis; we were 'en famille', and the discipline they exercised was in keeping with what would have been exercised at home by our parents. As pupils, the companionship we enjoyed was also an important contributory factor to our happiness at boarding school.

Chapter Ten

In addition to long school holidays, much longer than those enjoyed by children in the state sector, we had the additional bonus of lesson-free days on Holy Days of Obligation, Reverend Mother's feast-day and those of St Peter Fourier and Mother Alix. Most of these occurred during the summer term when the weather was warm enough for picnics.

One year a bus was hired on the feast of St Peter Fourier; the whole school, nuns included, went to Flamborough and we had our picnic on the beach at the North Landing. It was a truly happy outing and provided a rare chance for the nuns, particularly the Lay Sisters, to relax and have some fun, hitching up their skirts and paddling in the sea. The nuns sat apart from us to eat their packed lunches, for according to Canon Law they were officially an enclosed Order and were not supposed to eat in public; if any of us offered a sweet to one of them she would put it in her pocket to eat later.

Smiling benevolently, St Peter Fourier would have approved of the scene that warm summer's day. It was just such a family atmosphere he had wished for his schools. Technically the nuns were not keeping strictly to the law, as although they sat apart from us to eat they could still be observed, but the Founder had been a wise man and above stupidity. In his lifetime he had written to one of the Houses reprimanding the nuns because they had interpreted the Rule of Enclosure too strictly: in order to make a charitable visit to a home no more than a few yards away two of them had spent money unnecessarily on hiring an enclosed cab. 'On foot, on foot, in God's name!' he wrote. 'It is a sham, it is a new kind of I know not what bigotry thus to play at being scrupulous about enclosure, taking a carriage for that little journey, for fear of being seen or seeing, and yet, every three steps to climb in and out and pay visits.'

The spirit that he handed down to his nuns was essentially one of balance, leading to an absence of scrupulosity; therein, I am sure, lay the secret of our happiness among them as pupils and the reason why, as adults, former pupils are generally characterised by independence of thought, have a strong dislike of petty rules and bureaucracy, rebel against unreasonable authority and have none of the 'guilt' complexes that many other former Convent girls ascribe to their religious upbringing. St Peter Fourier himself had many battles with Bishops before he was allowed to found a monastic Congregation of nuns with the express purpose of educating girls-the first fully enclosed Order of nuns to do so. It was not until many frustrating years had passed that the nuns of the Congrégation de Notre-Dame were able to be called Chanoinesses de St Augustin.

A special treat on feast-days at school was 'bonbons de Notre Dame'. We had been told that these sweets were made from a secret recipe held by the Convents. I have learnt since, from nuns who came from other Houses of the Order, that it must have been a tradition peculiar to the House in Hull (or to the ones in France from which the Hull Convent sprang) for they had never heard of it! The recipe was in fact a simple one, the sweets being nothing more nor less than tiny meringues, slowly baked until they were brown. We thought them delicious and the mystique surrounding them added to their special quality.

For Reverend Mother's feast-day and that of Mother Hilda it was the Convent tradition that pupils put on an entertainment for the nuns. We threw ourselves into this heart and soul, organising the entertainment, finding scenes or sketches to act. We became adept at improvisations, which usually took the form of gentle, funpoking parodies of some aspect of school life. When the furore caused by the graveyard episode had died down, our form mimed the whole happening and it was received with much laughter. We had learnt from the nuns the valuable lesson of being able to laugh at ourselves and not to take life too seriously.

A perennial favourite in our entertainments was a sketch called 'The Obstructive Hat' pronounced "'at". It was about a little boy who had been taken to a pantomime and who could see nothing because of the large hat of the lady in front of him

'Ah can't see, muther, ah can't!' 'Lor' bless the boy, there aint nothing to see yet!' his mother replied.

We threw ourselves into the acting with gusto. Each time we performed the sketch the hat, bedecked with feathers, was made bigger and bigger, and more and more outrageous, and the audience doubled up with laughter. On the evening of a day when the Elocution Examiner had come to the school and stayed the night, we performed the sketch for her benefit after supper. I have not been able to trace the play since, and so wish I could; it was hilarious.

We loved acting, and one year the school put on for the parents a performance of a Japanese-style musical play called 'Princess Ju-Ju', directed by Mother Hilda. Wearing kimonos and with knitting needles stuck in our hair we revelled in it, unlike Mother Aloysia who had been detailed to provide the musical accompaniment. We thought the tunes were catchy, but she said the music was second-rate. In retrospect I realise that the words were dreadful too. The opening chorus began with the lines,

'Welcome to the Princess Ju-Ju!
Welcome to her sisters too-too!
Hearts full of joy,
Love sans alloy,
Welcome from her subjects true-true.'

However, the borrowed kimonos were pretty, Shirley Harris made a convincing Emperor, and June Tong a fetching Princess, although she has since said that Olive Leggott should have had the part, as the latter had a beautiful singing voice.

In better taste was a performance of J.M.Barrie's 'Quality Street' in which June Tong played the part of Miss Phoebe, looking very pretty in her blue, period costume. Previously it had been performed with Sheila Bacon in the part. Considering that the number of pupils was so small and we had no stage, only curtains hung between two of the pillars in the hall, we did remarkably well under Mother AElfreda's enthusiastic direction.

At the end of one term our form presented the first act of 'Les Voyages de Monsieur Perrichon' in French; this was produced by Mère Marie de l'Enfant Jesus, again with Shirley and June in the leading parts, and was very funny. True to character, we milked the humour to the last drop, delighting as ever in the audience reaction.

On a more reverent note, the Feast of Corpus Christi was both looked forward to and taken seriously. There was always, weather permitting, a procession of the Blessed Sacrament through the school grounds. The canopy and the richest cope were brought out from the sacristy, the children were sent to collect rose petals to be strewn before the Blessed Sacrament by the First Communicants in white frocks and rosebud wreaths, and there was much rehearsing of the hymns to be sung. Wearing white veils, we processed with the nuns behind the canopy under which the priest carried the Monstrance, and halted for Benediction at an outdoor altar, beautifully bedecked with flowers. The sweet smell of incense mingled with the heady perfume of the mock orange-blossom trees which were in full bloom. Raising fervent, joyful voices in praise and adoration, we sang the well-known and loved Latin words of 'O

Salutaris', Tantum Ergo' and 'Adoremus'. I remember as a young child in Hull once watching a Corpus Christi procession emerging from the gates of Endsleigh Convent near our house, and of being moved and fascinated by it. Perhaps the seeds of my early love-affair with Catholicism were sown then.

One of the most memorable of the 'jours de congé' we had at Boynton was that of V.E. day, the ending of the war in Europe. The war had seemed interminable, but when victory for the allies was finally in sight events moved rapidly. At last we knew it would be only a matter of days before peace was declared, and we set to work to build a massive bonfire. We had not been allowed to celebrate Guy Fawkes Days as that notable man had been a Catholic, but the bonfire for V.E. day more than made up for previous deprivation. On the top we placed an image of Hitler and on the night itself cheered and danced round the burning pile joyfully and ate potatoes baked in the embers.

It is perhaps a little difficult for those who did not experience the Second World War to understand the immense relief that news of victory brought; for those at home it foretold the return of those members of the Forces who had survived the fighting, as well as an end to food rationing and clothes coupons, to overall drabness, to travel restrictions; it promised a blessed return to normality. For six years people had prayed for the war to end, and it was only to be a matter of time before Japan was forced to surrender and victory for the Allies would be complete. The dropping of the Atom Bomb on Hiroshima some months later is still rightly spoken of as an act of inhumanity, but the cruelty inflicted by the Japanese on prisoners-of-war will not be forgotten either by those still alive who experienced it. V.J. night (Victory over Japan) was celebrated the following August in the middle of the school holidays. I remember going with my sister into the centre of Hull to join the ecstatic crowds. People were dancing, singing, cheering, hugging one another; it was a night that no-one who lived at the time will ever forget.

On V.E. Day I forget what else we did to celebrate, apart from being allowed to go into Bridlington, but I remember the day as being one of great happiness and in addition we were given the special treat of bonbons de Notre Dame!

Chapter Eleven

One of the advantages of attending a boarding school is that the life is well-regulated. This can of course turn into a disadvantage but in an enlightened school, such as ours was, the pattern can be broken occasionally, to the benefit of all. At Boynton we benefitted and grew from the treats and diversions, and absorbed the lifelong lesson that it is better to follow the spirit of the law than always to adhere strictly to its letter; if a regulation was found not to work well it was eventually abandoned, as in the case of the hated rest periods at weekends.

Much as we disliked these and the regulation walks, however, they did help to fill in time at weekends when there were no lessons. Children need to have their days well filled in order to prevent boredom; they also need to be reasonably supervised. On occasions when we were not taken for a walk, and after the rests were abandoned, some of the weekends seemed unbearably long, I remember. The nuns soon realised that, even though we welcomed Holydays of Obligation and Feast-Days as a break from lessons and routine, we did need to be kept occupied. Various activities were therefore devised on those days, such as treasure hunts.

On the whole we did not have much time in which to be bored through being at a loose end. During the week the two hours of supervised study filled in the time between tea and supper, and we went to bed at half-past eight. The period between supper and bedtime was usually a noisy one, when we let off steam, but frequently some activity was organised, such as Country Dancing or a film show given by one of the parents. One evening we saw 'Chu Chin Chow', and Maureen Matthews recently reminded me of how frightened we were when in the film a hand and arm rose up menacingly from the sand.

During the showing of the film 'The Song of Bernadette', we children were amused at Loffy's innocence when, as Bernadette said goodbye to a young man just before she boarded the coach that was to take her away to enter a Convent, Loffy said, 'Ees zat her bruzzer?' Although we were naive, we were a little more worldly-wise than she was!

The study period inculcated, in me at least, a need to study or write in an atmosphere of quiet; unlike many young people today, I cannot cope with background noise when I am needing to think. It also taught me to be able to concentrate. Similarly, regular mealtimes and bedtimes have remained a habit which I break to my cost.

At Boynton, chores were part of the regular pattern of our life, especially at weekends, though there was a period when washing-up rotas prevailed also throughout the week. One day I dropped a tray full of dirty dishes at Mother Hilda's feet but to my great relief all she said was, 'Oh dear, what a calamity!'

Saturday morning was shoe-cleaning time. Outdoor shoes and Wellingtons were kept in the Boot Room downstairs near the side door, for the rule of wearing indoor shoes was strictly enforced. We each had our own bag of shoe-cleaning materials and Saturday mornings saw us polishing and scraping, albeit reluctantly. I think later in the morning we had another period of study.

On Saturday evenings the usual study period was replaced by that of supervised letter-writing, during which we had to write home but could also write any other letters we wished to. There was a brief period when a few of us daringly corresponded with some of the Ampleforth boys, but as we never had a chance to meet them that soon died a natural death and Mother Hilda had wisely turned a blind eye. In any case, most of us were not really interested then in boys; we were quite happy without them!

On Sunday mornings the non-Catholics had to go to the service in the village church, some of us very unwillingly I'm afraid, and after tea, as on Fridays, there was Benediction. Between Benediction and supper we had Mending, supervised by Mother Hilda. Matron used to deposit on the table a large pile of lisle stockings, blouses, vests, socks, cardigans and knickers (the elastic of which was always breaking,) and out of our workboxes came wooden mushrooms, needles, thread, thimbles, navy wool, buttons, bodkins and cards of elastic. Having collected our own particular pile of clothes to be mended we set to work but not with a will! During Mending, Mother Hilda read to us, which helped to relieve the boredom of a chore that most females hate. Life for me was not made any easier by the fact that my clumsy darning was sometimes compared unfavourably with the meticulous sewing for which my sister had been renowned at school.

The nuns took it in turns on Saturday and Sunday evenings to take us for Recreation, and there was a period when Mother AElfreda read us a detective story as we gathered round her by the log fire, avidly listening. Our favourite was 'Murder in a Nunnery', a battered copy of which I still possess. Written tongue in cheek, it was so true to Convent Boarding School life and we readily related to Verity Goodchild and her battles with Mother Peagle, who acted more in sorrow than in anger!

Immediately before bedtime we were led into chapel for night prayers; these finished with a prayer for the 'faithful departed' and I regularly intoned, 'and may the petrol light shine upon them'; it was not until I saw the words in print one day that I realised I should have been saying 'perpetual'.

Twice a day we said the Angelus, at midday and at six in the evening. When the Angelus bell rang, our lesson or Study was immediately suspended whilst we stood at our desks and recited the prayers. If Loffy happened to be taking us the prayers were said in French, as was Grace before and after meals. I doubt whether any of us can ever forget the words of the Grace, indelibly imprinted on our minds:

'Au nom du Père, et du Fils et du Saint Esprit. Mon Dieu, bénissez la nourriture que nous allons prendre pour réparer nos forces, afin de vous mieux servir. Au nom du Père, et du Fils et du Saint Esprit.'

Religion was never thrust down our throats; it was just there, a normal and accepted part of our lives. References to God, to praying, along with private visits to the chapel, were made unselfconsciously and without any embarrassment, and I think it was that above all which attracted me so strongly to the Catholic religion (for at home God was kept for Sundays, and even then hardly mentioned, except when I had to say my nightly prayers) although it was not until very many years later that I finally decided to convert.

Our physical, as well as our spiritual, health was taken care of on a routine basis. After breakfast and at bedtime the medicine cupboard was opened, and at night we were, if necessary, dosed with sennapod tea. There was always a large jug of it looming menacingly before our nostrils and it was something we submitted to with bad grace: it tasted as foul as it smelled. There was a period when Matron decided we should all gargle each night with salt and water, but we quite enjoyed this once we became proficient; we learnt to make tunes with our gargling and the corridor then echoed to the sounds of our efforts, each of us vying with the other in variety and proficiency.

Bedtimes were usually strictly adhered to, and in any case we were tired by the end of the day and ready to sleep soundly, but every so often the villagers asked if the senior girls could attend a Beetle Drive in the Village Hall. Why they kept inviting us it is hard to say, unless it was to swell the ranks, for we refused to take the drives seriously. 'Beetle!' one of us would shout out triumphantly a few minutes after the drive had begun, having outrageously cheated. 'Them Boynton 'allers!' the villagers would exclaim, half in frustration and half tolerantly.

Usually our consciences were able to justify slight deviations from strict honesty (such as denying having talked in the dormitory when we had stuck our heads out of the window to do so) but in the matter of cheating I can, on looking back, find no real exoneration, except that it was never done for personal gain! We all used to cheat when marking one another's sliptests in Latin, giving each other eight out of ten when nought would have been nearer the mark. Normally we were honest and fair, and deviations from the norm can, I suppose, be put down to the fact that we took neither the Beetle Drives nor the sliptests seriously.

Our daily life was well balanced between work and play, rest and exercise, normal rowdiness and quiet, discipline and freedom, serving and being served, familiarity and respect, religion and secularity. Looking back, I can see that our life at school was regulated rather than full of regulations, contained rather than restricted; surely that was largely the secret of the nuns' success.

Sincerely loyal to the school, and sincere in our affection for the Convent and the nuns, we were also loyal to our Houses in a way that would, I think, be foreign to the more sophisticated children of today. When I first arrived at Boynton I was claimed by St Thomas

More's House and (giddy heights of responsibility) eventually became its House Captain.

There was great rivalry between the Senior Houses of St Thomas More and St John Fisher, each competing with the other in the matter of Order and Merit Marks and on the games field. Letting the House down was considered by us to be a serious crime, and although the House system may be scoffed at today it inculcated virtues and values that nowadays so often seem to be lacking. We learnt self-discipline and responsibility; we also learnt from the example of the nuns how to wield power, when it came our way, with fairness and humanity. I have never felt that the competitive spirit inculcated by the House system is to be decried, provided that it is kept under control and that children can learn to be good losers.

Once, we were invited to a concert at the Village Hall and were greatly diverted by a recitation given by one of the village youths. He recited a poem by Rudyard Kipling:

'The camel's 'ump is an ugly lump which well you may see
    at the zoo-oo-oo,
But uglier yet is the 'ump we get from having too little
    to do-oo-oo!'

On the whole it cannot be said that we at Boynton Hall carried that hump, or any other, on our backs. Even Matron's treatment of me personally, damaging as it was, loomed less large than it might have done, because the other girls shared my dislike of her and I had their sympathy.

One of the really good aspects of our school life was, with one notable exception, the goodwill that prevailed among the pupils. There was no nastiness, tale-telling, verbal abuse, quarrelling or character-shredding; there was enormous companionship, highlighted by the lack of it that I felt at home, and the one threat mother could effectively use was to take me away from the Convent. The fact, however, that we were indeed far from being saintly can be illustrated by our treatment of one of the girls in our form who didn't fit in.

Children can be merciless and in this case we were no exception. The girl in question unwittingly broke the code that says 'Thou shalt not be different.' Very tall and shy, withdrawn and awkward, also older than we were, she didn't join in with us even though we did our best to persuade her to do so and she was never deliberately left out. We tried teasing her, and she reacted by becoming more withdrawn and unhappy and our behaviour then became rather unkind- to my great shame and, I know, to that of the others.

One day we were fooling about in the classroom, throwing the chalky, cotton board-duster at one another whilst our 'odd one out' remained at her desk and took no part. In an effort to include her in the fun we threw the duster at her, expecting her to throw it back at one of us when all would have been well. When she didn't react we turned on her and pelted her with the duster.

Having myself been on the wrong end of bullying (at the hands of adults) I can relive with her the agony she will have felt and can sympathise with her inability to handle it and fight back. It was unfortunate that, being so much older than we, she had to be in the same form as we were, for our general behaviour must have struck her as puerile! Because she was the oldest among us the nuns felt they had to make her Head Girl the year before she left school; it was a well-meaning gesture but not in that case a wise one; her lack of natural authority made her position all the more untenable. Our own contribution to her unhappiness was inexcusable, but in our defence it can be said that we did initially try to make her one of us.

Chapter Twelve

The girl who was the odd one out became so only because she felt inhibited from joining in. Others of the pupils were different in other respects but fitted into the whole in a prevailing atmosphere that allowed for, and accepted, differences. Although we were at an Independent School, there was no snobbishness nor any reason for it: on the whole our families were not well-off, nor did we come from the higher echelons of society.

About a third of the girls were Catholics; the rest of us, apart from Shirley Harris who was Jewish, were referred to as the Protestants, or Non-Catholics; we saw no reason to be offended by this. Shirley was excused prayers, services in chapel and Scripture lessons, but the Protestants were required to go with the Catholics to Benediction on Fridays and Sundays (probably because there would have been no-one left to supervise us) although not to attend Mass; nor did we have to attend catechism lessons. On reaching Confirmation age we went regularly to the Vicarage to receive instruction from Mr Lawrence, the dear old vicar who was so kindly and erudite. We were confirmed at Rudston, the village where Winifred Holtby, the author of 'South Riding', is buried.

Some of the girls came from homes where spoken English was less standard than that of the majority of us. They were not made to suffer on account of this, but one of them caused great amusement in the Elocution lessons her parents paid for. Chronically unable to aspirate her aitches, she tried Mother AElfreda's patience to the limit:

Mother AElfreda: Mary, say "Harry, hang your hat on the hook in the hall."

Mary: 'arry, 'ang your 'at on the 'ook in the 'all.

Mother AElfreda: Try again: "Harry, hang your hat on the hook in the hall."

Mary (after a deep breath): 'arry, 'ang your 'at on the 'ook in the 'all.

At least a place could be found for her in the Yorkshire sketches we loved to perform.

One term a girl arrived at the school bearing the aristocratic name of Julia Grimstone, of Grimstone Garth; this intrigued us but otherwise was of little consequence: it added only to the diversity. We were not made to conform to a set pattern or moulded into anything artificial; there was no pretentiousness or pretence, just simplicity and with it quite a lot of naivety, but I don't think that was such a bad thing. Although it didn't fully prepare us for the real world on leaving school, it was preferable to suspicion and cynicism, precociousness and mistrust, and unlike many other former convent girls we did not go off the rails once we had left.

As well as diversity of religion and social class there was a variety of nationalities. The small community of nuns comprised those of French, German, English and Irish origin. Later among the children there were French girls, an Estonian called Tiu Mannapso, and three Polish refugees with initially unpronounceable names. The latter brought the war nearer to us, for they had horror stories to tell of life in Poland and their flight from the Nazis.

Stationed near Boynton for a while were some Polish soldiers; they used to be marched to Mass in our chapel on Sundays and the non-Catholics among us would stand outside the door and listen, for the soldiers raised their voices and sang in a way we had never heard

63

before; it was an experience not dissimilar to hearing a Welsh male-voice choir.

In a room near the chapel lived Mrs Tolhurst. Auntie Tollie was an old lady, one of the paying guests, and we used to make excuses to knock on her door and pay her a visit, for she always gave us two toffees each to go away with. Occasionally Dot Oxley's soldier husband was granted leave and the two of them then rented rooms in a cottage in the village. They once kindly and thoughtfully invited some of us to tea, and we arrived to find a laden table. We did justice to the tea, and appreciated being able to relax afterwards in an atmosphere redolent of home, amusing and entertaining Dot and her husband with lively accounts of the scrapes we got up to. In contrast to their kindness and tolerance, my godmother who lived nearby in Bridlington never once invited me to tea or took me out; she had disapproved of my being sent to a Catholic school.

Among the white-veiled Lay Sisters were two who were actually sisters, Sister Marguerite and Sister Agnes, both Irish. Sister Marguerite was round and rosy-cheeked and lovely. After Soeur Joséphine's death she did the cooking until she died in 1949, and although much of the food was spoilt she did occasionally turn up trumps and produce something delicious. The Lay Sisters, who did the housework, were fully professed but unlike the Choir Nuns (whom we addressed as 'Mother') were not obliged to say the Divine Office; this the others had to recite five times a day, and I used to love to hear their chanting.

Soeur Joséphine had died soon after my arrival at Boynton, and Soeur Henriette was very old and not able to do very much. Sister Agnes and Sister Imelda were strong and active but there was a shortage of hands to do the housework and Mother Aloysia took it upon herself to do the bulk of the washing-up. The sight of little

Buggy in her blue apron and with sleeves rolled up as she tackled the horrid porridge plates convinced us of her sanctity, but we did wryly say that when she reached Heaven she would go around switching off all the lights there.

Lights were a constant battle between Mother Aloysia and the other nuns. Conscious of the need to economise, Buggy used to switch off any corridor light that was on, leaving us to feel our way in the dark, a task made more hazardous because of the uneven flagstones; the other nuns would switch the lights on again! The real battle royal usually took place between Buggy and Loffy; there was no love lost between the two of them- the one very English, quiet and well-bred and the other very French, loquacious and volatile.

Mother Gertrud used to come out from Hull once a week with the clean washing! It was her task to put us to bed on Matron's night off and what a blessed relief it was! Taking the opportunity to read her Office whilst supervising our ablutions, Mother Gertrud rarely noticed our misdemeanours. One night these included standing in the enamel washbasins on top of the lockers to wash our feet, instead of on the floor; she probably and wisely pretended not to notice, and our childish prank fell flat. When we were in bed Mother Gertrud came round and tucked each one of us up tightly. The nuns were indeed motherly, and even when Mother AElfreda, more like a sister to us, occasionally put us to bed, she left us with a comfortable feeling of being cared for by blessing each one of us on the forehead with the sign of the cross.

Chapter Thirteen

One day Mother AElfreda called our form together and told us that Reverend Mother had asked her to start teaching us plainsong, in order to help the nuns in Hull to sing Mass on feast-days. Some of the older nuns such as Mother Franciska and Mère Marie Ange had died, and the community at the French Convent had had to be split during the war when the boarders moved to Boynton. Reverend Mother Philomena had remained at Hull along with the Mère Assistante, Mother Cecilia, Mother Gertrud and Mère Marie de la Presentation, who taught the few day-pupils still attending the French Convent. As the building in Park Grove was occupied by the army, the pupils were taught in the Manse, one of the four houses in Pearson Park owned by the Convent. The Lay Sisters who remained in Hull were Sister Gabriel, Sister Bridget and Sister Angela who was the 'Externe'. She was the only one officially allowed outside the Enclosure in order to do the shopping, and wore a distinctive fringed veil. With so few Choir nuns, Sung Masses had had to go by the board until Reverend Mother thought of enlisting our help.

As only one or two of our form were Catholics, the rest of us were asked if we would mind taking part also. We took no persuading, for the prospect of a night spent at the Hull Convent was exciting.

After supper we began to gather regularly round the grand piano in the Music Room, under the malevolent eye of the wicked Sir Walter, to learn the intricacies of Gregorian notation and the rhythm of the cadences, and at last we were pronounced ready. In our best uniforms and with overnight bags packed, we set off early on a Saturday evening in the battered old Wolsley with Mother AElfreda at the wheel. The excitement of such journeys was enhanced by her willingness to drive ever faster at our urging and by the car's propensity to 'wheel wobble'; today it would not have had a chance of passing an MOT!

At first our high spirits were temporarily subdued on arrival, for we were in awe of Reverend Mother and, unlike the Hull girls who took it as a matter of course, felt awkward about the tradition of having to curtsey to her. Furthermore, the formal Convent parlour at the nuns' house, Willersley, was far removed from the shabby but comfortable room in which visitors were received at Boynton. We were not too happy either about encountering Spiv, the Bulldog that Reverend Mother had inherited from Mother Dorothea!

On our first visits we were allotted bedrooms in Southside, where the nuns had paying guests, but once the soldiers had departed from the school building (having ruined the beautiful oak staircase with their hobnailed boots) we slept in the large dormitory. We loved this, for we each had a cubicle to ourselves, white-curtained and with a locker. To us this was luxury. We were unsupervised, we had the building to ourselves, and there was no question of keeping silence. Left to ourselves our normal ebullience returned.

Southside housed permanent paying guests including Mrs Richardson, Mother AElfreda's mother. Most of them had been there for many years and seemed quite formidable. We had supper at Southside and breakfast the next morning after Mass. Slightly overawed, we sensed the disapproval of the elderly inhabitants who were not used to having schoolgirls in their midst. However, we made the most of the unaccustomed luxury of being able to toast our bread at the old-fashioned gas fire, and of eating food cooked by Sister Gabriel which was of a notably higher standard than that served at Boynton. On extra special Feasts we were served at breakfast with warm, freshly-baked brioches and a generous portion of butter. After that we were allowed to visit our homes until Mother AElfreda was ready to return to Boynton.

On one of these visits home I found that my mother's friend from Halifax was staying there. She and mother had arranged to go for a trip to Bridlington for the afternoon on the bus. A dreadful scene ensued because my mother wanted me to accompany them instead of returning in the school car, and I flatly refused. Journeys in the school car were a highlight of our schooldays and I didn't want to miss the fun. Mother was hurt, and perhaps began to regret having sent me away to school; I had begun to identify too much with the Convent and was patently happier there, where I was beginning to find myself, than I was at home.

The gulf between home and school widened as I continued to absorb all that appealed so much to me about Catholicism. Going to the Hull chapel to sing High Mass even during the holidays (I remember a group of us also went carol singing around Pearson Park one Christmas Eve) became a regular occurrence and I came to love the ritual and the beauty of plainsong. We learnt to sing not only the more commonly known Missa de Angelis but also the lesser known ones and finally graduated to the more difficult chants used in the Proper of the Mass. We also sang Requiem Masses for the nuns who, sadly, died whilst we were pupils at the school.

The Latin Requiem Masses were beautiful. The solemnity of the long Dies Irae was offset by the hope contained finally in the In Paradisum, 'May the angels lead you to Paradise', sung with ineffable sweetness as the coffin was borne out of the chapel. We were allowed to accompany the nuns and relatives to the burial in the Catholic section of Hull Cemetery, and to gather round the grave as the last rites were performed. I came away better for the experience. I saw nothing maudlin, frightening or distasteful: death was seen to be a natural ending and a new beginning.

Life is a matter of constantly learning and growing from new experiences, and it was on the evening before the first of the Requiems we attended that I came face to face with the physical reality of death. We had been told that if we wished we could go into the chapel to see the body and it was an experience that removed from me any fear of dying.

The chapel seemed eerie, the darkness dispelled only by the light of the tall candles at the four corners of the open coffin, and the comforting, red glow of the sanctuary lamp. Kneeling in the shadows was one of the nuns, taking her turn to watch and pray. With some trepidation my companion and I approached the low bier near the sanctuary and looked on Sister Marguerite, lying there dressed in her Habit. Around the head was the circlet of white rosebuds worn by her when she made her profession, and in between the folded hands was the paper witnessing the Vows she had made. Life had patently left the body but the facial expression was one of great peace and repose and I felt very moved and awed.

At Requiems there is always sadness at the loss of someone loved but other occasions when we sang at Mass in the Hull chapel were joyful ones. The Clothing of a postulant some years later was one such occasion, although there was a certain piquancy in seeing the bride, Kathleen Morris, walk down the aisle without a groom.

For us the occasion was especially meaningful, for Kathleen was the same age as we were and had come to Rise as a pupil-teacher; formerly she had attended the Ladies of Mary Convent at Scarborough where Mother Hilda had been educated. It was not long before she decided to enter our Convent. As the number of

Postulants during and after the war had declined, this gave us an unforeseen chance to witness a Clothing, particularly in the form such a ceremony took in the days before the Second Vatican Council.

It was with some excitement that we gathered in the chapel at Hull, filled with Rise Girls, Kathleen's relatives and the full Community of nuns. At the point in the ceremony when the Postulant was led away to be clothed in the habit, we curiously awaited her return as Sister Alexia, wearing the white veil of a Novice. We imagined meanwhile the scissors being wielded to cut her hair, although we knew that, contrary to the practice in many Orders at the time, it wouldn't actually be shaved! After the ceremony we were able to speak with her briefly, and on visits to the Hull Convent always managed to have a few words. It was lonely for her in the Noviciate, and she was pleased to be able to converse with young people again for a few minutes.

For the Convent, a Clothing was a joyful occasion, but for us Midnight Mass was especially joyful. Each year, those of us who lived in Hull cycled to the Convent through the empty streets late on Christmas Eve. The beautiful chapel, brilliantly lit, with its white altar of Carrara marble massed with candles and flowers, now had the addition of a large Crib. When the Convent clock chimed and then struck the hour of midnight, Reverend Mother placed the image of the Infant Jesus in the previously empty manger and the symbolism of the Nativity began.

Afterwards we gathered happily in the Cloister before going to Southside where the large dining-table had been laid for us with a light repast. By the side of each plate the nuns had placed small presents of home-made confectionery, beautifully wrapped, and there was also a little gift and a Holy Picture for each one of us from

Mother AElfreda. I still have the thimble that was her gift to me one Christmas, as well as the many Holy Pictures given to us at various times by the nuns, including one from Loffy, written in French, for the occasion of my sixteenth birthday. My old Latin Missal is crammed full of them- a nostalgic reminder both of school and of pre-Vatican Two days, and also of the affection the nuns showed towards us.

To her credit, my mother tolerated all this, I think because it didn't enter her head that I would ever 'turn Catholic'. My sister had passed through the nuns' hands without anything worse than an attraction towards Catholicism that never reached fruition, and mother no doubt thought that I too would come through unscathed!

St. Pierre Fourier

L'âme qui est en état de grâce est belle, pure, nette, plaisante, agréable à Dieu et en chemin pour aller en paradis.

St. Pierre Fourier's autograph

Alix le Clerc

Alix le Clerc:
autograph manuscript

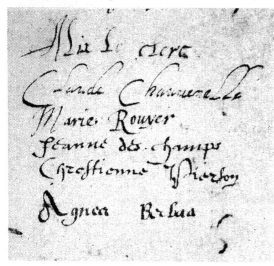

Boynton Hall, July 1994
Gypsy Race in the foreground
(The white door was the one in the Big Dormitory)

Rise Hall, front entrance

ST. PHILOMENA'S   RISE, SKIRLAUGH

1948

Kneeling: Gillian Nettleton, Vivienne Moore, Margaret Prociuk, Lesley Wood

Sitting: Beata Braun, Marylyn Jones, Marie Sherburn, Jane Wight, Gillian Sutcliffe, Sally Long, Wendy Spencer, Ann Lamplugh,
Stephanie Prescott, Maureen Matthews, Jean Bancroft, Brenda Hastings, June Davidson, Zoe Watson, Valerie Frazer,
June Rutter, Shirley Spencer, Julia Grimston, Ann Watson, Valerie Charlton

1st row standing: Carol Fargus, Sally Fenton, Gillian Hall, Judy Loton, Jean Goswell, Josephine Shaw, Jennifer Reader,
Mary Marr, Valerie Fisher, Margaret Edwards, Jean Crossland, Kristina Dobrascinska, Hanka Less, Janet Loton,
Judy Hatton, Dorothy Gaze, Diana Robinson, Ann Giovetti, Gillian Stather, Beryl Marnock

Back row: Judith Cate, Betty Marr, Martine Waldron, Zoe Euston, Dorothy Kirby, Victoria Lincoln, Ann Ainsly,
Gillian Spencer, Susan Ripley, Elizabeth Hughes, Anne Chester, Brega Bassett, Penelope Grimston,
Jean Massey, Ann Brown, Helen Massey, Christine Tune

School photo, Boynton Hall, 1946

Mother Hilda with 'Trinket' at Rise

Mother Aloysia, (Buggy),
and Perdie, 1949

Mother AElfreda
in the mid 1960's

Mother AElfreda and myself

Hanka Less: baggy shorts!
Rise, 1949

Loffy, Rise:
'summoned by the bell'

First day at Rise:
Mother AElfreda, Mr and Mrs Sherburn
and Marie

Mother Philomena

Three stooges: Janet, Stephanie and myself, swotting for exams
during the heat-wave of 1950

Sister Imelda, Sister Gabrielle and Sister Agnes

Lac d'Artouste, 1948
Mother AElfreda, Maureen Matthews, Brenda Hastings
and Kathleen Morris (Sister Alexia)

Rome 1950: yellow berets in the foreground

Fire practice, 1950

Making hay with Mother Hilda and Matron Nerney

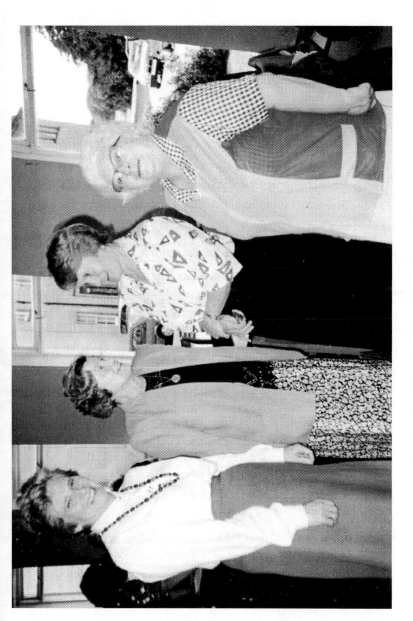

Jennifer Hart, Dorothy Kirby, Jill Stather and Joyce
Rise OGA Reunion, September 1994

Chapter Fourteen

I have always been thankful that the bulk of my secondary schooling did not take place in a modern building. The historical character of Boynton was ever present to us in the ancestral portraits of the Strickland family and many things reminded us that the Hall had once been someone's home. In our classroom downstairs in which there was a beautiful carved stone fireplace, the shelves lining the walls were filled as in the Big Dormitory with old, much-thumbed, calf-bound volumes of varying sizes. The Hall itself was not very large or imposing but every brick and stone spoke of ages past, as did the previously mentioned priest's hole, secret passage and the Gypsy Race.

There were many corridors and several staircases, along which we were taught to stand aside to let an older person pass, and one afternoon a couple of us ventured up the narrow stairs that led to the unlocked attics. There we found a treasure trove: among discarded pieces of furniture and paintings were tin trunks full of ancient letters and family memoirs. Fascinated, we read some of the letters, the ink faded and the paper yellow with age, and went back again several times. One of the good things about Boynton was that doors were not locked against us, although certain boundaries were set; we never, for example, ventured uninvited down the corridor where the nuns slept, or through the green baize door that led to Father Reilly's quarters.

The Convent had its own age-old traditions and we were proud of their uniqueness. Not for us the labelling of forms by numbers; ours were labelled from E to A. The lowest form in the Senior School was C2, the next highest was C1 and so on through B2 and B1 (the School Certificate class) until A2 and A1 were reached by those of us who stayed on to sit for the Higher School Certificate.

When I joined the school I was placed in B2, moving up to B1 with my older classmates and twice repeating the year; I did virtually the same syllabus three times which did me no harm and meant, at least, that I had a thorough knowledge of the particular period of History that we studied for School Certificate when I finally came to sit the examination!

The game of Reserve that we played was, I believe, unique to the Convent, as were the Stride and the Norwegian Ladder in the gymnasium at Park Grove. Unique also was the original colour of the uniform, slightly brighter than the normal navy-blue, although when war came the manufacturers were no longer able to produce the 'Mary blue' dye and specially made gymslips, box pleated but with a pointed yoke, that my sister and her contemporaries had worn; we had to make do with navy blue and with ordinary gymslips instead.

Another casualty of the war was the old-fashioned black sateen overall that completely covered the uniform beneath, with sashes going around the waist and over the shoulders, of a different colour according to each form. At Boynton the overalls were replaced with 'scapulars' made from blackout material and we hated them, although they served their purpose in protecting our uniforms in the days when material had to be dry-cleaned. The sashes were retained (but tied round the waist) and designated not our forms but the House to which we belonged: red for St Thomas More and blue for St John Fisher. The scapulars consisted of a long, straight piece of material with a large hole cut out for the head, and tied at the waist with black tapes. When the sashes remaining from pre-war days had petered out they were replaced by an elasticated belt of the type that was popular when 'wasp waists' were fashionable. We, however, looked anything but fashionable and frequently 'forgot' to put on our scapulars, although this rarely escaped notice. The traditional, old-fashioned overalls would have been more becoming.

We were proud of our school colours, blue and gold. Until the war the blazers had blue and gold twisted braid round the edges and I was able to wear the one that my sister had kept from her schooldays. The school crest on the pocket of the blazers was in the form of a gold cross and a white lily (the emblem of St Peter Fourier) on a blue background. Formerly there were badges made of enamel, a large one for the hat band with a smaller version to pin on our ties, and I still have these in my possession, handed down to me by Dorothy when I first went to Boynton. The exercise books and rough books bore the school emblem, but these too became a casualty of the war.

We were quite proud of the straw boaters that were part of our summer uniform when I first went to the school, although they were the cause of many a battle with authority. We felt they looked unbecoming when placed flat on our heads and we used to tip them back only to have them tipped forward again when we were inspected before setting out. Once out of sight we tipped them back again! They were a nuisance, too; if we happened to be sitting in a bus in Bridlington the local boys who sat behind us tipped the boaters hard on to our noses. One girl's boater blew off into the sea one day and I don't think she was sorry to watch it bobbing away on the waves.

Most former convent schoolgirls will remember collecting money for the Black-Babies. Each form had a poster pinned to the wall on which were printed thirty wide steps. At the bottom were pinned paper black babies, one for each of us, and each time we contributed a penny our black baby could move up a step. When an individual contribution had amounted to half-a-crown and the top step had been reached we were allowed to name our baby, the chosen name supposedly being sent to the Missionary Society. I hope the poor children were not in fact saddled with the outrageous names we devised, such as Claetemnestra Anastasia.

At our school we traditionally had an annual holiday from lessons when we held a 'Black-Baby Day'. Each form spent days beforehand thinking up an original way to raise money for the Mission and much ingenuity was brought into play. The form that raised the most money was given a prize. When the school moved to Rise, where there was a very long cellar, our form devised a Ghost Train, using a large wheelbarrow as transport. Reverend Mother came to 'the Gypsy Encampment' (as she called Rise) for the day and surprised us all by allowing herself to be wheeled in it. She was flapped at by white-clad figures, had a clammy sponge pushed against her face, her ears were assailed by ghostly music, shrieks and wails, and her eyes by luminous skeletons. We were impressed by the fact that 'Queen Victoria' was such a good sport.

The Ghost-Train was so successful it was repeated year after year. At a recent Reunion some of us went down into the cellar and found skeletons and skulls still there on the walls where we had painted them. It was even exported to the school in Southern Rhodesia where I later went to teach.

Speech-days were not part of our school tradition, but Prize-Giving was. It took place at the end of the Christmas Term, and was always followed by an entertainment put on by the pupils for the parents. The nuns and priests sat in the front row, the parents behind them, and the pupils sat at the back if they were not performing, neat and tidy for once and without scapulars!

At the end of the Christmas term also it was traditional when I was at school for a post-box to be erected, covered in red crepe paper; in it we posted the cards we had spent hours beforehand preparing for the nuns and for our friends; the classrooms reeked with the smell of the ink eradicator with which we blotted out the writing on old Christmas cards brought from home. There was great excitement when the post box was opened and the cards distributed.

At Pentecost Mother Aelfreda gave at random to each of our form a little picture she had drawn herself, depicting one of the Gifts of the Holy Ghost. On Easter Sunday, after those of us who lived in Hull had helped to sing High Mass at the Convent, there by our plates at Southside were little home-made nests containing tiny Easter eggs. In these ways, with due proportion, we shared with the nuns in the joyful celebration of the great Feasts of the Church. The sacred and the profane were linked and the latter gave meaningful expression to the former.

There was always a balance. Even Lent was not allowed to become burdensome. Encouraged though not forced to make some kind of sacrifice, most of us gave up sweets, but were told that we could have them on Sundays as that was a feast-day. This was a very Catholic and French way of regarding the Sabbath, a day in which special praise was given to God in a liberal spirit of joyful thanksgiving. Religion was not made too onerous for us.

An end-of-term tradition we shared with many Public School boys was that of 'quis?' and 'ego'. When we cleared out our desks we could rid ourselves of unwanted items by saying 'Quis?' ('Who wants it?') and someone was sure to reply 'Ego!'(I do!') This happened throughout the year but at the end of term it reached gigantic proportions.

As soon as we reached home at the beginning of the school holidays we were expected to write a letter or postcard to Mother Hilda, telling of our safe arrival and thanking her and the nuns for having looked after us during the term. This was a rather unnecessary and unspontaneous practice which originated with Matron, noted for taking things too far, and ended with her departure, but genuine courtesy, thoughtfulness and politeness had traditionally been a notable and fundamental part of the education provided by the nuns.

If we met Reverend Mother or passed her in the corridor we had to curtsey; that traditional form of respect may seem quaint to modern eyes but it certainly did generations of French Convent girls no harm to observe. Tiny, dignified and imperious, but also kindly, understanding and in many ways wise, Reverend Mother resembled Queen Victoria not only in stature but also in demeanour and, indomitable as ever, she lived to the age of a hundred and one. It is my own belief that part of the reason for her longevity lay in the fact that she made a practice of never standing when she could sit.

One of my most vivid remembrances of Reverend Mother Philomena was on our visits to Hull. We always went first to Willersley, where we waited in the Parlour for her to come and greet us. Overawed by the surroundings we used to speak almost in whispers until the door opened and her small, dignified, erect figure appeared, her face wreathed in smiles. She always seemed tolerantly amused by us. When she had seated herself on one of the elegant 'Louis Quinze' chairs, we were invited to sit down whilst she chatted to us briefly. Once dismissed from her presence, we fled in relief to resume our normal ebullience. At the end of our visit we once again went to Willersley and waited in the corridor by the front door. Before long she would appear from the door at the far end and sit down on the long, low bench by the wall whilst we stood to receive her farewell words. It was on one of these occasions that she told us of the practice she made of sitting whenever possible.

The old lady was very much a part of the old tradition, although she was able in many respects to move with the times. After her funeral, when we were looking round the graveyard at the resting places of the other nuns I had known so well, I remarked that they would all be up there saying, 'Watch out; here she comes!' Mother Philomena was, however, held in a great deal of affection and had been particularly loved by the French Convent children and those who had lived closely with her at Hull, for although imperious she had a sense of humour, was interested in life and in people and never forgot any of the pupils who had passed through her hands. I think one of her best qualities was that, although she believed that one should try not to shock others she herself was unshockable; this made her tolerant of human error and understanding of human weakness.

In two respects, though, she refused to move with the times. One was her refusal to surrender autonomy and join the Union of the Congregations; the other was her retention of the medieval habit when after the Second Vatican Council the nuns were given permission to discard it. Along with one or two of the lay Sisters she retained hers to the end.

The habit worn by the Canonesses, identical to that seen in the pictures of Mother Alix, the co-foundress, was a simple but attractive one. Rooted as it was in the past, I believe it contributed to the comfortable feeling of agelessness and security we were given when at school, as did the French terminology that had been retained; it was, after all, known as the French Convent. The black, white-lined veil of the nuns' habit was placed over the white linen 'guimpe' that framed the face and hid the hair; the term 'wimple', the English equivalent of 'guimpe', was not known to me until I came to read Chaucer. For Divine Office the nuns had long, warm, choir cloaks and wore an additional thin, black veil.

As the habits began to wear out they were beautifully darned or patched. The French Convent had always been noted for beautiful sewing, but when I was at school I'm afraid the pupils failed to maintain that particular tradition, although we greatly admired the sewing and needlework done by some of the nuns. Loffy used to do beautiful drawn-thread work (and tried without much success to teach us to do the same) and I remember watching Mother Gertrud with admiration as she sewed by hand a trousseau for a former pupil. I cannot understand why our sewing lessons with Mother Gertrud took the form of endlessly learning how to patch sheets; I never did master the art and have certainly never put it into practice since then!

In the parlour at Hull there was a glass-fronted cabinet displaying items of the nuns' work, offered for sale. There was also a large photograph album containing pictures, mostly postcards, of the Convent at Versailles before the nuns had been forced to flee. From the pictures we could recognise most of the furniture in the parlour at Hull, along with the French beds we slept in, and were fascinated by the grille in the Grand-Champs parlour, a reminder that officially our nuns belonged to an enclosed Order. Hanging in the parlour was a portrait of Queen Marie Leczinska, wife of Louis XV and daughter of the King of Poland, which she herself had given to the nuns. She had come to know the Canonesses in 1767, when the Court was at Compiègne where they had a convent and school, and was appalled at the poverty in which they were living. She became their patroness and on the death of her father she decided to use her inheritance to build them a new monastery at Versailles. She had been shocked by the corruption and decadence to be found at the Palace there, and wanted a good, Christian school for daughters of the courtiers to attend.

Marie Leczinska died the following year, but her husband, her daughters and the Dauphine Marie-Antoinette, continued to take an interest in the project and in 1772 the 'Couvent de la Reine' was completed and a new school was founded. The children's uniform had been designed by the daughters, Adelaide, Sophie and Victoire, and it was Madame Adelaide who drew up the school timetable. At first there were seven boarders but by Christmas many more had joined them, along with two hundred day pupils.

Unfortunately in 1772, during the French Revolution, the school had to close. The nuns had refused to take the Oath of Allegiance to the State and were forced to leave the concent and abandon the religious habit, although none fell victim to the Terror. In 1804 the people of Versailles begged them to return. The Couvent de la Reine had been confiscated but the nuns acquired Grand-Champs in the Rue Royale and within the first few months there were ninety pupils. During the nineteenth century the number of nuns in the Community rose to around sixty.

In 1904 disaster struck once more in the form of renewed anticlericalism and the teaching Orders were expelled. The nuns, having with foresight requested permission of the Bishop of Middlesbrough two years previously to settle in his diocese, came to Hull. They had managed to transport over the Channel many items of furniture and priceless possessions, including the portrait of the Queen.

At first they settled at 5 Albion Street with eight pupils, but soon bought four houses in Pearson Park and drew up plans for a school to be built behind these in Park Grove. This was completed in 1906 and became known as The French Convent. Mother Philomena was received as the first English postulant in that same year, and ten years later became Headmistress a position she retained until 1972.

The long history of the Order is an interesting one and, admiring its spirit as I did, I always felt proud to be a part of it.

Chapter Fifteen

'Le zèle de l'instruction est le sujet de ma vocation.'

Alix le Clerc

The spirit of the Order and the nuns' consequent success in the field of education can be traced to the nature of the Congregation's foundation and to the character of the two Founders.

When the Canonesses first came into being in 1597, it was due to the indomitable spirit and vision of a young girl, Alix le Clerc, and her parish priest, Père Fourier. Convinced, along with Alix (whose burning desire was to lead a monastic life) of the need for girls to be educated, Pere Fourier met with seemingly insurmountable opposition from fellow priests and the Vatican, for the Rule of Enclosure upon which the Vatican insisted was thought to be totally incompatible with the idea of teaching. Himself a Canon Regular of St Augustine, he wished to found an Order of unenclosed nuns closely allied with his own expressly for the purpose of teaching, free of charge, any girl, rich or poor, who sought education. (The children of families who could afford to pay were charged a fee for boarding but not for tuition.)

When permission to found such an Order had finally been granted (although within the Rule of Enclosure), those who had joined Alix in the monastic life under Pierre Fourier's direction were at last, after twenty years, allowed to be professed and take formal vows of Poverty, Chastity and Obedience. To the latter a fourth one had been added: that of a vow never to allow the work of education to be neglected; in this the Order was unique.

The Canonesses sprang from very small beginnings when, after initial reluctance on Pierre Fourier's part (for he wished to test the aspirants' sincerity), at Midnight Mass he formally recognised Alix le Clerc and her four young companions as a religious Congregation. They had already been working and praying together and had adopted a simple, uniform style of dress. They were named The Congregation of Our Lady.

At first there were many difficulties; the nuns found it hard to make ends meet and lived in very real poverty, and there were personality clashes between Mother Alix and Pierre Fourier. The former underwent great sufferings, including tests of humility when, no longer allowed to be Superior, she tried hard to please and to adapt herself to the rule of another. She had great spiritual struggles, but her sanctity became obvious and eventually led to her Beatification. Although she had clashed many times with her co-founder, the latter had a great admiration for her, recognising her virtue, steadfastness and drive. It is interesting that on her death in 1622 it is recorded that Pierre Fourier used white vestments, not the purple ones of mourning, when he conducted the Requiem Mass; this seems to indicate that he already recognised her sanctity.

Before the death of Alix many other Houses had sprung from the original foundation at Mattaincourt, and by the time of Pierre Fourier's death in 1640 there were fifty convents in Lorraine and France, for the education given by the nuns was much sought after. These spread quickly to other countries. However, difficulties had multiplied also. Père Fourier had wanted all the Congregations to be joined together in a Union, under a Mother General and with one set of Constitutions. This met with strong clerical opposition and some of the convents refused to accept the Constitutions he had drawn up for them. Until the death of Alix, however, there was a form of unity in the loyalty shown to her by the original Congregation and others who had joined it.

It was not until three centuries later that a move towards Union was made. In 1897, the year Pierre Fourier was canonised, Rome officially recognised the Union of Jupilles, comprising mainly the Houses of Belgium and Brazil. In 1926 the Houses in France were made into a simple Federation. This became the Union Romaine in 1931 (interestingly for me the year of my birth) and by 1963 it had thirty-six monasteries and eight hundred nuns. The two groups finally became a single Union in 1963, thus fulfilling the wishes of Pierre Fourier; it included, with one or two exceptions, all the Houses in the Order except ours for Mother Philomena stubbornly refused to join it.

Why Reverend Mother refused to join the Union is not clear. Perhaps it was because of her autocratic nature and the fact that she had been Superior and in sole command since 1920, with only two nominal breaks of three years each when Mother Assistante officially, though not in reality, took her place; perhaps, on the other hand, it was because she was fiercely proud of the line of descent from the House at Soissons and did not wish it to be dissipated by amalgamation with the other branches of the Order. It was a line she herself had furthered by her own subsequent foundations.

The French Convent in Hull, autonomous and virtually cut off from the other Houses in the Order, was the Mother House of its three offshoots Meudon, on the outskirts of Paris, Boynton (later Rise) and a small foundation near Pau in the Hautes-Pyrénées. Mother Philomena had founded the Meudon House in 1936. The nuns there had once again to abandon the habit when war broke out, but the school flourished and does so to this day. The one at Béost was later to close, and kindly Mère Therese (known to generations of pupils as 'Monkey-Face'), along with a protegé, Solange Medevielle, and rosy-cheeked Sister Catherine, came to Hull.*

When Mother AElfreda eventually replaced Mother Philomena as Superior, one of her first acts was to join the Union. This meant that the dwindling number of nuns could be augmented by those from other Houses, and that money could be directed from a central source, thus making it possible to redecorate and smarten up Rise Hall; it also happily healed a rift. This happened, however, many years after I had left school.

Times have changed and in the Western World teaching Orders no longer attract many postulants; in the poorer countries, however, the Order still has many new entrants. Today the total number of over eight hundred nuns can be found in countries as far apart as Algeria, Zaire, Mexico, Hong Kong, Vietnam, Belgium, France, Hungary, Italy, Holland, Germany, Austria, Luxembourg, Czechoslavakia and Brazil, as well as Great Britain. Although the precise nature of their work and life has in many cases changed with the times, they still continue their teaching apostolate in various ways and in accordance with the spirit of the Founders.

The character of our education at the Convent, which had sprung from small beginnings, was due originally to the vision and gentleness of St Peter Fourier. As well as being a saintly and much loved parish priest, he was an outstanding educationalist and, like all visionaries, was ahead of his time. Perhaps the first feminist, he thought that girls had as much right to education as boys had and 'perhaps, because of their influence in society, were more in need of it.' Such a view is at last being promulgated by forward thinkers in the Third World today. Supremely well-balanced himself, Pierre

Fourier was kindly and understanding and saw the need for discipline to be tempered with kindness and for learning to be pleasurable: the nuns under his direction were exhorted to treat the children in their care with gentleness and good humour.

The following instructions given to the nuns by Père Fourier sum up the spirit of the Order and that of the education given by the Canonesses:

He said that an extension of the teaching of religion was insistence on 'politeness and good manners in movement, word and actions'...The pupils' behaviour should have nothing in it of 'vanity, arrogance, affectation or notable oddity, but should conform to the standards of good courteous Christians living in the world'...The teaching of goodness had to be done 'gently, discreetly and opportunely, as occasions and capacities serve, so that (the children) become good workers, as far as possible, and as it were habituated or naturalised by practice...The mistresses will use prudently all kinds of opportune occasions to exercise their pupils either all together, or in small groups, in all the above mentioned' (virtues and devotions) one being that the pupils should not curse their brothers and sisters, nor strike them, nor use hurtful words; another, that they should never tell lies, or speak evil of anyone 'but always without forcing them, and without too much urging, and not boring them or being importunate.'

He said that there was to be no softness in the government of the school, that right authority had to be obeyed and that the mistresses 'will above all recommend promptitude and punctuality in obedience...The Mother Prefect will never allow a formal and evident disobedience or any self-will to go unpunished' but, in keeping with his own spirit, he also knew the need for firm discipline to be tempered with gentleness...'The teachers must have for their pupils a pure and sincere affection in mind, actions and words. For the inculcation of the Christian virtues they should choose the gentlest and easiest way, which best takes account of their weakness.'

With regard to the academic side of the nuns' apostolate, Pierre Fourier said that teaching should in general be done 'always gently, so that the tender minds of these children are not overburdened, or wearied, or deprived of appetite for that good food...The teachers must not be cross or angry with those who have difficulty in learning, but must exercise patience and gentleness, make allowance for them, and encourage them lovingly to do their best...they must try in all things to treat them with great gentleness and a perfect motherly love...patiently putting up with their little weaknesses...so that they know they can always run to their mistresses with complete confidence and without fear whenever they want.'

Pierre Fourier was also ahead of his time in the ecumenical field. Referring to the Protestants among the pupils, he wrote in 1624:

'If amongst them there is a girl of that supposed religion, treat her gently and charitably, and do not allow others to molest her, or reproach her or quarrel with her. Do not openly invite her to abandon her error, and say nothing directly against her religion...And if they learn well, you may praise their diligence and their good work, and give them as prizes, instead of pictures and "Agnus Dei" that you give the Catholics, gilt paper or a good pen, or suchlike things that they would not scorn.'

'Do good to all, do harm to none,' the motto of St Peter Fourier, adopted by the schools, was the basis of our education as a whole and left its imprint on generations of pupils. Where outside influences within the school as I knew it were at odds with this spirit, the harmony was disrupted and for that reason they were eventually replaced by those who were able to follow the principles set down by the founder.

On looking back, it is possible to see how these principles formed the main thread of our education. We were brought up to be 'ladies' in as much as politeness and good manners were instilled in us, and little acts of courtesy such as offering to carry books for our teachers, to stand up when they entered a room, to stand aside to allow another person to pass, and to speak politely (I was once reprimanded for saying 'Bye bye' to one of the nuns) became second nature. Politeness did not, however, mean that we could not speak freely; we conversed on terms of equality with all, no matter what their status; neither was there any fawning, bowing or scraping, nor conception of being 'yes-men', and behaving like ladies did not mean that we were falsely ladylike; most of us were in fact tomboys.

The fact that the pupils were not all Catholics meant that we grew up in an atmosphere of tolerance and respect for the religion of others; there was no bigotry or wrongful indoctrination. Ecumenism reigned at the convent long before the Second Vatican Council; we were aware of differences but saw one another as people, not as 'Catholic', 'Protestant' or 'Jewish'.

The simplicity and lack of affectation extended into the realm of the spiritual. There was no false piety, no hands raised in horror if one of us dared honestly to express feelings of hatred for the Matrons, but we learned imperceptably to behave charitably towards others and not to detract wrongfully from another's character.

The gentleness and sympathy we encountered as pupils meant that we could without fear report our feelings to others and not be forced unnecessarily to keep a stiff upper lip; it also meant, on the other side of the coin, that we were not really trained to encounter unfriendliness in the world on leaving school. The spirit of the Order fostered independence and determination but not the emotional toughness needed for coping with the lack of gentleness and kindness encountered in Western society; we were certainly not brought up to be 'street-wise'! The answer is surely not that our essentially Christian education was wrong but that society; needs to learn the lessons that we were taught and to become courteous, kind, gentle and therefore harmonious.

With regard to the period before Rise Convent joined the Union, I think it fair to say that these principles were in fact reinforced by the separation. In a non-material way the latter had almost certainly played a part in the creation of the family atmosphere at Hull, Boynton and Rise, and had also contributed to our feeling of security. Because the nuns were not moved away, we came to know them well, they were still there when we visited them after leaving school, and there was a comfortable feeling of continuity.

As pupils we were aware of the separation from the Union and had been told something of the Order's history. We had heard of 'Les Oiseaux', the name of one of the Houses of the Roman Union, in the Rue de Sèvres at Paris. It was from there that the nuns had fled to Westgate-on-Sea in 1904 and had founded a flourishing school. The name of Westgate and also that of St Leonard's, another of the English Houses founded at that period, were mentioned quite frequently by Mother AElfreda, and we were intrigued to know that there were other nuns of the same Order, wearing the same habit, following the same Rule and presumably possessing the same spirit and also other Convent girls probably very much like us. We would have liked to meet them. This was not possible at the time, although it finally became so in Rome at the Beatification of Mother Alix in

1948. (By an irony of fate I have, forty years later, come to know one of my contemporaries from Westgate, now Vicar Provincial of the English Vicariate of the Order; she tells me the food at Westgate during the war was very good in stark contrast to ours at Boynton!) I myself could not go to Rome in 1948 but an opportunity did arise, though, for visiting Meudon.

* Interestingly, and not surprisingly to those who knew Mother Philomena well, the Houses she founded did not have separate Mother Superiors, only nuns placed in charge. There was only one Reverend Mother and she was not going to relinquish control!

Chapter Sixteen

One of Reverend Mother's first acts when the war in Europe ended was to visit the House at Meudon in the summer holidays, and Maureen Matthews and I were invited to accompany her. I looked forward with excitement to my first visit abroad.

Mother and Dorothy did their best, at short notice and with limited resources, to fit me out with clothes. During the war few new clothes had been bought for me; most of the days were spent in school uniform (it was not until many years later that the boarders were allowed to wear home clothes at weekends), which used up precious coupons, and in the holidays I was dressed for the most part in clothes handed down by my grown-up sister, or in a skirt topped by jumpers I knitted for myself. In any case, shops did not cater for teenagers.

The clothes with which I was sent to France were by no stretch of the imagination becoming. In addition I was encumbered by a wide-brimmed, totally unsuitable, straw hat. Maureen, whose father took an interest in her clothes, was far better turned out. I could tell that Reverend Mother was not impressed with my appearance but there was little I could do about it!

Once we were at Meudon, Maureen and I were left to our own devices. As the boarders were on holiday, we had the large school building to ourselves, sleeping in a huge dormitory not unlike the one in Park Grove. We ate at one of the several nuns' houses in the grounds, and attended Benediction and Sunday Mass in the tiny chapel there.

Mother Magdalena, the nun in charge at Meudon, kept a motherly eye on us, and we made friends with the Convent goat, ate

90

the apricots picked for us from the orchard by Mère Marie de Gonzague, and sat on a bench in the part of the garden that overlooked the Seine. We never tired of the wonderful panorama of Paris, dominated by Montmartre and the gleaming white Basilica of the Sacré Coeur. I have in my home a reminder of the scene in the form of an oil painting done many years later by Mother AElfreda.

Having been starved of fruit during the war, we revelled in the apricots that abounded at Meudon, and we bought and devoured the peaches that were everywhere on sale. Food, in fact, became a major preoccupation! France had hardly begun to recover from the German Occupation, and the nuns apologised for the hard, black rye-bread we were served but we quite enjoyed it. Everything was a novelty and we instantly fell in love with France. I also loved the faint aroma of garlic and Gauloises cigarettes that seemed to permeate Paris.

At first two of the boarders who lived locally were detailed to show us around, but soon we were allowed total freedom to go where we wished in the vicinity and to take the train into Paris to the Gare Montparnasse. That station stands out in my memory on account of the shop there where we bought packets of dry meringues to consume on the train journeys back to the Convent.

Maureen and I became expert at finding our way about Paris and at using the Métro. Loffy's expert teaching of her native language, together with her custom of speaking to us in French, stood us in good stead. We visited all the sights and loved the Palais de Versailles and the Trianons; we revelled in the hot summer sun but relished the coolness to be found in the Bois de Boulogne, the cathedrals, the Louvre and other monuments; we sat in the Jardins de Luxembourg and wandered around the Latin Quarter. We were only fourteen years old at the time, but the fact that we had to find our own feet on our first visit to a foreign country was not at all alarming; having learnt at school to be independent, we took it in our stride.

The wanderings around Paris were punctuated by my need to seek out patisseries where we could drink tea (weak and revolting, served with boiled milk which left bits of skin floating on the top) and eat delicious French pastries: rhum babas, coffee éclairs, meringues filled with cream, almond cakes and other such delights. My blood sugar dropped continually, probably as a result of the unaccustomed intake of sugar in the form of fruit and pastries, and Maureen was very patient over my need to find a patisserie before I fainted in the streets of Paris. I had already fainted one morning during Mass in the hot, airless chapel.

Chapter Seventeen

Life at Boynton came to an abrupt end. In 1946 the ownership of the Hall that the Convent had rented since 1934 passed into the hands of a distant relative of the Strickland family and the lease was terminated almost at a moment's notice. Mother Hilda and Mother AElfreda spent the summer holidays frantically touring East Yorkshire for new premises, and unable at first to find anything suitable they were obliged to postpone the opening of the new term.

It was with great sadness that we said goodbye to Boynton for the last time, and we went home not knowing where we would find ourselves in the autumn. An epoch was over and life was to change. Still a happy one, it was never again to be quite as relaxed and happy-go-lucky as it had been at that lovely Elizabethan mansion in which we had spent so many carefree days.

In September 1946 the school moved to Rise and, once the nuns had settled in, was reopened for the autumn term. The move from Boynton to Rise, as recounted by the nuns, had been in retrospect hilarious, with a convoy of forms of transport of varying shapes and sizes, including a truck on the back of which were the hen-coop and its occupants, who clucked and squarked indignantly.

Naturally we pupils were greatly excited, but most of us felt that Rise Hall was disappointing in comparison with Boynton. Apart from the fact that it was badly in need of redecoration and repair, that the roof leaked and the central heating boiler constantly broke down, the building was Georgian not Elizabethan (therefore less romantic!) and seemed to us architecturally somewhat stark and forbidding; furthermore there was neither a priest's hole nor a secret passage! In a way it symbolised what was to come: the change in our schooling which thenceforth became more serious in nature, though the original spirit remained.

As a building, Rise Hall was far more suitable for a school than Boynton had been; it was larger and, when the central heating worked, slightly warmer! The grounds were not extensive but beyond the boundary of the gardens there was a large park with two lakes; these were overgrown with weeds and dangerous and we were content normally to keep our roaming within the actual precincts of the school.

The grounds provided ample space for our needs, although they were overgrown and untidy. Everything about the Hall indicated neglect due to lack of money: paint was peeling, the outbuildings were falling into decay; there was little glass left in the conservatory; the gravel paths and cobbled courtyard were full of weeds, and although there was a tennis court it was unusable and we had to do with a makeshift one on the grass at the south side of the Hall. However, as the school's reputation began to spread, such things did not deter parents from sending their daughters there; they opted for a happy atmosphere rather than for smart and comfortable surroundings.

Unromantic as the Hall seemed in our eyes, it had some redeeming features. There were beautiful, Italian style, ceilings and carved stone fireplaces, and an elegant, sweeping, wide and curved principal staircase. Some of the ancestral portraits remained on the walls, reminding us of the stately-home nature of the building, and there was a large library, shelved all the way round from floor to ceiling. Best of all, in our view, were the old-style lavatories. These were set in a wooden structure on small platforms, and in one of the bathrooms there were two side by side! We named the lavatories 'Country Seats'.

The two bathrooms with their old-fashioned washbasins and baths were a great improvement on the washing facilities at Boynton where we had no actual washbasins at all. There were still only two baths, at which we had to take our turn once a week, but eventually a shower was installed and new basins were put inside cubicles in the bathrooms, affording us some privacy at last. The days of trying to strip beneath our dressing-gowns had gone for ever.

The war was over and despite its dreary and unforeseen aftermath everyday life gradually began to improve. For us, one of the first signs was that eventually the squares of newspaper hanging by a string in the lavatories were replaced by toilet paper; this was an improvement but no longer allowed us an excuse for lingering! However, we did begin to have access to news from the outside world, for Mother AElfreda saw to it that papers were delivered to the school; these were placed on the round table in the hall outside the Butler's Pantry. Determined to enjoy ourselves, we quickly settled in. I was aware that School Certificate was drawing nearer but decided that I would take life fairly easily before settling down to hard work.

Chapter Eighteen

One of the first changes that occurred when we moved to Rise was in the uniform. Under Mother AElfreda's increasing influence the unbecoming navy-blue pleated gymslips were replaced by skirts worn with white blouses and blue and gold striped ties, the summer boaters by Panama hats and the winter navy berets by specially designed golden-yellow ones. The latter were distinctive, although we didn't care for them very much, as were the old-gold best dresses that Mother AElfreda had designed. These looked attractive but were impractical as, being made of moygashel, they were not easily laundered and they were abandoned soon after I left school. However, along with the berets they served a very good purpose when some of the pupils accompanied the nuns to Rome for the Beatification of Mother Alix in 1948 and again for the Holy Year of 1950; it meant that they were easily distinguishable in the huge crowds! (One of my contemporaries has remarked that perhaps we should now call ourselves 'the Golden Oldies'!)

It was a great relief to us when the navy-blue frocks we had to wear on Sundays in winter were abandoned; these had detachable white collars which we had to remove for laundering and sew on again. I could never get mine to sit straight, and even when I resorted to press-studs instead the result was not very satisfactory. The pleated, navy-blue shorts, however, that we wore for P.T. and Games were not replaced by more practical ones.

As with the skirts (and previously the gymslips and dresses) the shorts were of a regulation length. The hem of the skirts had to touch the ground when we were in a kneeling position, and the shorts had to come only a few inches above the knee. As they were also wide-legged they were not at all practical for athletics. Doing the High

Jump necessitated tucking the hanging pleats into our elasticated knicker legs as best we could. It was not a very aesthetic sight.

After the move to Rise, the school became firmly established in its own right; it was no longer just an offshoot of the French Convent in Hull, necessitated by the war. When the school in Hull was able to move back into the original premises in Park Grove, it no longer received boarders but continued to cater for the growing number of day-girls. Parents who wished their children to board formed the overwhelming majority of pupils at Rise, where the only day-girls were a few who lived locally. Thus the need was felt to provide Rise Convent School with a name that would distinguish it from its parent in Hull and yet retain the link. The name chosen was St Philomena's after Reverend Mother Philomena.

Several years later, after the Second Vatican Council, it came as somewhat of a shock (as well as a source of amusement to us) to be told that our particular Saint had been struck off the register. Apparently there was no proof that she had ever existed. Although the name of the school was officially retained until then, its religious demotion made little difference for we were always referred to by others as 'Rise Convent'; the original name had already died a slow death.

There was, blessedly for me at least, a change of Matron soon after we moved to Rise. Matron Nerney was sharp-tongued at times but never sarcastic and, unlike her predecessor, was a trained nurse, practical and sensible, and had no fetish about fresh air and regular dosing. She hailed from County Cork in Southern Ireland, had a sense of humour and a relaxed and not over-serious approach to life, and she was directly instrumental in restoring my self-confidence and in giving me a sense of my own worth.

Taking people as she found them, Matron Nerney liked me and I gradually lost my shyness with adults and began to blossom. We became good friends, and under her influence Mother AElfreda regarded me in a new light, her previous prejudice dispelled. A true friendship then began to develop between us, one which lasted until her premature death in 1977.

The change in the attitude of Mother AElfreda, whom I had always liked and admired, in spite of the fact that she allowed herself to be dominated by those who had a more masterful personality, gave me the added boost I needed. My real development as a person, and also academically, dates from that time. I had an absorbent mind and my general outlook was widened, first through the many conversations Matron Nerney and I had together and then, as our friendship grew, by those I had with Mother AElfreda.

Matron's worldly-wiseness complemented the simplicity of the Convent atmosphere and taught me much that, being virtually an only child, I was unable to learn from home where my mother and sister were preoccupied in other ways. Mother AElfreda, on her part, became a source of inspiration to me in so many ways. Her own broadminded and no nonsense approach, as well as her youthfulness and charismatic personality, her sense of fun and unconventionality, did much to help me through the difficulties of adolescence. As I grew increasingly unhappy at home she gave me sustaining and understanding help and acceptance, and was someone to whom I could always turn for sympathy, advice and companionship when I needed a means of escape long after leaving school.

For me, the move to Rise, with the changes it brought, had come at an opportune time. Sadly for the Convent the nuns were growing older and the Lay Sisters fewer. Pupil numbers were increasing and lay staff were employed to help with the teaching. Among these was

Joan Ingram who had been in the same form at Park Grove as my sister; she came from the Hull Convent once a week for Games. This meant that in hockey and netball we improved considerably and began to play matches against Filey Convent. We even won occasionally, which was a considerable achievement, for the number of pupils at Filey far outweighed the ones at Rise.

During an inter-House netball match, watched by the nuns, I remember once in exasperation saying 'Damn!' on missing a shot at the goal, and was reprimanded by Mother Hilda. Relaxed though our schooling was, we were never allowed to use even the mildest swearword; the four-letter words used so commonly today were of course totally foreign to our ears and we would certainly not have understood their meaning; (we had been left wondering about what happened at Sodom and Gomorrah!)

Mrs Holmes was recruited from the village along with her son, Geoff, and daughter-in-law, Joyce, to help with the manual work; they became an indispensible part of the establishment and helped to alleviate the shock to the local village community caused by the sudden arrival in their midst of nuns and ebullient girls. Startled at first, the villagers came to shed preconceived notions about Catholics and Convent Schools, and this was due in large measure to the inside presence of Mrs Holmes and her family. Neville, who later replaced Geoff Holmes at Rise Hall, told me not long ago of his surprise on first entering the place when it was still a school; he had expected, on a Sunday afternoon, to find the children sitting quietly and was amazed to have his ears assailed by the loud hum of voices and by boisterous sounds emanating from all parts of the Hall. He had nothing but praise for the school; and confessed to me that, had it not been obliged to close, he would have sent his own children to be educated there.

Mrs Holmes who, at the time of writing, is in her nineties, eventually retired but Joyce remained, even when Rise Hall no longer operated as a school, always welcoming and pleased to see us when we returned for Reunions. She remembers every face and name going back over a period of fifty years and having identified with the school and become so much a part of it she truly embodies the 'Rise spirit'. She is now, at the time of writing, the only one remaining there of the original inhabitants, a rock of stability for those of us for whom the original stability of the nuns was of such importance in our development. When the nuns move out of Rise Hall, and we have our reunions elsewhere, I think I would be speaking for all the Old Girls were I to hope that she would join us.

The changes brought about by the move to Rise proved the truth of the adage of its being an ill wind that blows nobody any good. The recruitment of qualified teaching staff was of course beneficial to our academic education, and that of Mrs Holmes and her family meant that we no longer had to help with the household chores!

Chapter Nineteen

Among the villagers at Boynton we had been known as 'Boynton Hallers' and the school had not been very well known outside Hull and Bridlington. It was at Rise that it began to acquire a reputation for excellence and we gradually became well known as 'Rise Girls'. Individualistic as ever, somehow we were stamped with something unique and intangible, hard to put a finger on or to name. At the funeral of Mother Philomena in June 1989 one of the priests who visited the school regularly said to me, 'Rise girls are different from any others I know.' When I asked in what way, he found it difficult to explain but thought that perhaps it was because of their unselfconscious directness and their capacity for simple enjoyment.

I believe some of that was due to the spirit of the Order, whereby we were encouraged to be open and friendly with our teachers of whom we were not afraid, and there is no doubt that the pupils under the care of the nuns learnt to have independence of mind, integrity and self-respect, as well as a caring concern and respect for others but at Rise especially our full, individual potential was nurtured and allowed to come to fruition. This had the effect of giving us confidence in our own abilities and the absence of a need to push ourselves forward or consciously to impress others. With no fear that we might be 'put down' we became accustomed to thinking for ourselves and expressing our own opinions, and we were totally at ease in our surroundings, and with others who accepted us for what we were. When former Rise girls come together we immediately feel at home and relaxed with one another, no matter what the difference in age; we are rather like members of a family who have been brought up together, for there is a shared ethos.

The spirit handed down by St Peter Fourier is presumably to be found in all the convents that had accepted and retained his

Constitutions; our schooling at Boynton and Rise was not unique in this, nor was that of the Convent in Hull. However, the fact that 'Rise Girls' came to mean something special was due, I am sure, to the great influence and vision of Mother AElfreda. After I had left school she became the headmistress but for some years before that she had been the real driving force behind the kindly but ageing Mother Hilda.

At Boynton, our happiness at school was due essentially to the wise rule of Mother Hilda, but after the move to Rise when Mother Hilda gradually took a back seat it was mainly due to Mother AElfreda that we continued to be so happy and to flourish. Under her influence and tacit holding of the reins the régime was both tightened up and broadened. Gaps in the academic side of our education were filled by hook or by crook and Mother AElfreda's efforts were well rewarded. The school achieved a reputation for character-building as well as for academic success (with eventually thousands of O Levels and hundreds of A Levels to its credit, and with several of the pupils later passing the Oxford Entrance Examination) as well as success in other fields, whilst the relaxed, unstuffy and happy atmosphere remained unchanged.

At Rise Mother AElfreda worked tirelessly to restore the former reputation of the Convent, previously damaged by the scandal caused by Mother Dorothea. Under her direction our minds were broadened, our education was widened and our eyes were opened to the outside world. We retained our former simplicity but became less naive. In all this she had the support of Reverend Mother (who still kept a watchful eye on the Gypsy Encampment from her throne in Hull!) and who herself came to rely more and more on Mother AElfreda, of whom she was especially fond. Much of the former's precious time was, in fact, taken up by Reverend Mother's constant need of her presence, either physically in Hull or over the telephone.

After I had left school, and at the same time as she was virtually in charge at Rise, Mother AElfreda also resumed the degree course that had been interrupted when she entered the Convent. At the time when I was doing my postgraduate Education Course at Hull, she began an eighteen month London University External Correspondence Course; this meant studying mostly by herself, with help from two of my former tutors at the University: Rosemary Woolf and Rachel Trickett. She and Miss Trickett became very good friends and when the latter moved shortly afterwards to St Hugh's College, Oxford, the link between herself and Rise was happily maintained, with former pupils going up to St Hugh's to read English. Mother AElfreda herself had obtained her English Honours degree, but all the strain she underwent, together with lack of adequate rest, began to take its toll on her health, which had never been robust.

On being elected Superior several years later, Mother AElfreda displayed a practical genius for organisation with regard to the running of the Convent and for making difficult but important decisions. After the closure of the Convent in Hull because of structural unsoundness as a result of the war, a house was found for Mother Philomena at 99 Newland Park, off Cottingham Road in Hull, where she could live quietly in retirement, looked after by Mère Marie de la Présentation and Mother Gertrud, and attending Mass at the nearby Marist Church.

Although Mother AElfreda was already Superior, the seat of government thus moved to Rise in name as well as in reality. The French Convent, so fondly loved and remembered by all its former pupils, had ceased to exist and Rise Convent, once an offshoot, had become the English Vicariate's House in Yorkshire.

Reverend Mother AElfreda, (known by then, like all the nuns, as Sister) was, like her predecessor, at the same time Superior and Headmistress. She had lost none of her drive and vision, and worked tirelessly in all directions, but her health was finally stretched to the limits. Sister Alexia was necessarily occupied in studying at Hull University at Sister AElfreda's instigation, but the latter fortunately had excellent support in Mrs Swannick whom she had made Deputy Head. When cancer was finally diagnosed early in 1975 and Sister AElfreda had to give in to her last illness, Mrs Swannick became Headmistress, with Sister Alexia (who obtained her Theology Degree in that same year) as Deputy Head.

After the death of Sister AElfreda, who had been Headmistress for twenty years, there was a period of two years without an official Superior and Rise was under the direct jurisdiction of the Vicariate. Sister Emmanuel, who had come to the school a short while before, helped with the running of affairs until Sister Geraldine, who had been Vicar at the time of Sister AElfreda's death, was free to come to Rise as Superior. Mrs Swannick retired and Sister Geraldine took over as Headmistress. It was she who had the sad task in 1989 of finally having to close the school for which Mother AElfreda had laid the strong foundations.

When we first went to Rise, Mother AElfreda was still full of youthful vitality, and the only indication of the way she was driving herself lay in the migraines from which she constantly suffered. She was full of ideas, and part of her vision for the future had been a desire for a purpose-built School Hall and Gymnasium. With the support and help of the parents a fund was set up and the vision eventually became a reality. It was tragic that Sister AElfreda died without being able to see the fulfilment of her dream: the Hall which we as pupils had all longed for and which bears her name.

Chapter Twenty

On first moving to Rise, life had soon settled into a gentle routine of work, play, prayer, games, walks, mealtimes, early to bed and early to rise, but the routine was soon to be disturbed. In the winter of 1947 came the big freeze-up.

Few who lived through it will forget those long weeks when the country was blanketed in deep snow. We were blocked off from the outside world and supplies ran low. I remember some of us tramping across the park and the fields with Matron Nerney, trailing a sledge and falling into snowdrifts in order to reach the shop at Skirlaugh. There we loaded the sledge with provisions before attempting the long tramp back. When supplies ran dangerously low, one of the fathers came with a van-load of provisions.

The roads were piled six feet high on either side with snow that had been cleared by as yet un-repatriated German prisoners-of-war. When Father Reilly died suddenly it was a question of how the body could be borne away for burial in Hull. The coffin was in fact taken to the road leading to Whitedale Station, strapped on to sledges. The gravediggers at that time must certainly have earned their money!

The flat countryside of Holderness made tobogganing impossible and the novelty of the first snowfalls, in January, very soon wore thin. By the end of that seemingly endless term we were all heartily sick of the sight of snow and the restrictions it brought, and felt as we had done about the war that it was going to last forever.

However, Spring at last returned; the lilac trees in the garden came into bloom and inspired Mother AElfreda to think about producing 'Lilac Time' for the Christmas Entertainment. Charmed by the story and by Schubert's music (this time approved of by Mother Aloysia), we fell in with the idea enthusiastically. Lilac-coloured material was bought (or perhaps it was white muslin dyed) and Matron Nerny spent many hours at the sewing machine; other costumes were to be hired. My services were required as assistant accompanist at rehearsals and I spent many hours at the piano practising the musical pieces. At rehearsals I had to rush from piano to stage, alternating between acting and accompanying. In a school so small, although by then the numbers had risen to the region of sixty-five, we were well versed in the art of versatility!

Once rehearsals had begun the building echoed to the tune of 'Tilli and Willi and Lili Weit' and the strains of 'Yours is my Heart'. It was not easy for Maureen Matthews, playing the part of Schubert, to sound suitably romantic but the final performance was well acclaimed, due allowance having been made for the fact that male characters had to be portrayed by girls.

Rise, like Boynton, was naturally not equipped with a stage. The musical was performed in the Front Hall, curtains having been rigged between the pillars at one end. At the far end, lighting had been set up by one of the fathers. When, fired by the success of 'A Midsummer Night's Dream' and 'Lilac Time', Mother AElfreda produced 'Daddy Long-Legs', we were able to present the performance on a proper stage in the large gymnasium at the Hull Convent, where we had begun to hold our prize-givings. As Rise was much nearer to Hull than Boynton had been, it was a simpler matter to transport the whole school there in the bus that was regularly hired for outings.

Loving sentiment as we did, 'Daddy Long-Legs' had always been a favourite of ours, both as a book and a play. We had performed it once before, at Boynton, with June Tong and Shirley

Harris unforgettable as Judy and her guardian. The orphanage scene especially will live forever in our memories.

The second time the play was performed, I took the part of Daddy Long-Legs, with Marie Sherburn playing Judy Abbott. It was not a part I enjoyed; my acting talents lay more in the field of comedy and my old self-consciousness returned, causing me to gabble my lines. Mother AElfreda had a difficult task trying to make me speak them more slowly, I remember.

Although I have trodden the boards many times since then with my local Dramatic Society, no longer self-conscious, I could not in a million years hope to emulate the success of Sarah Bernhardt. However, one of the pupils who came to Rise the year that I left was determined to make acting her career, and appeared several times in television plays. Anna Palk's rather tempestuous personality as a pupil was indeed reminiscent of that of the 'divine' Sarah, as was her great love for the school and special affection for Mother AElfreda. Tragically, her career was cut short; after a long and painful illness she died not long after the school closed. The last picture I have of her is of painfully struggling along on crutches, when the Old Girls came together for the grand reunion that marked the school's closure.

Most of us were avid readers and, whilst literature lessons successfully instilled a love for the classics, owing to the enthusiastic and inspirational teaching of Mother AElfreda, reading for relaxation took the form of devouring the romantic novels of Georgette Heyer. We read every one of them, although 'These Old Shades' and 'Friday's Child' were our favourites, and our conversation for a time became punctuated with expressions such as "Lud!" and "'Pon rep!" We also loved the 'Berry' and 'Bertie Wooster' books, laughed our heads off at 'Three Men in a Boat', shed tears over Ernest Raymond's 'Tell England' and were romantically carried away by the Bronte sisters and Jane Austen.

We scorned girls' school stories, with the exception of 'Dimsie', much preferring books about boys' schools such as 'Greyfriars' and 'Tom Brown's Schooldays'. On a recent visit to Boynton Hall I was interested to learn that the eighth Baronet, Sir Charles Strickland, is said to have been the model for the character of Martin in 'Tom Brown's Schooldays'. That provides a fascinating and hitherto unknown link between Boynton and Rise!

As in the case of the novels we read, we wallowed for a time in sentimental poetry. Rupert Brooke was a favourite among us and I can still recite by heart almost the whole of 'The Old Vicarage, Granchester'. My party-piece at Elocution was 'The Soldier' ("If I should die, think only this of me...") which was infinitely preferable to the one I formerly had very self-consciously to recite: 'Have you ever heard the wind at night go "Whoooo"? 'Tis a pitiful sound to hear!' A poem that I loved and that still haunts me was 'The Quarry': "O, what is that sound that so fills the air, Down in the valley drumming, drumming?" Reverend Mother once remarked, rather disapprovingly, on my penchant for pathos!

On the Fine Arts side, our cultural education was limited to the ancestral portraits until we visited Paris, Florence and Rome, where we feasted on Leonardo da Vinci, Fra Lippo Lippi, Michelangelo and Raphael. However, Mother AElfreda did once borrow from the Library an art book to show us, containing pictures of the Great Masters; this was done in a sensible effort to allay silly schoolgirl giggling at nudity by showing us that the human body could be beautiful and not a cause for embarrassment. This lesson served us in good stead when we came face to face with the original works in France and Italy.

Chapter Twenty-One

In 1948 a few of us went again to France, with Mother AElfreda and Reverend Mother. The latter remained at Meudon whilst we went with Mother AElfreda to the Hautes-Pyrénées to stay with the two nuns who were living in an ancient chateau in the Basque village of Béost. We had a marvellous time.

Well accustomed to physical deprivations, we were in no way dismayed by the conditions at the Chateau de Béost. The primitive lavatory in the garde-robe leading from the room in which we slept was merely a hole in the outer wall; we had moved back several centuries in time. The village too still belonged to a former age; many of the older inhabitants were dressed in the 'costume du pays' and spoke only in patois. They were friendly and anxious to speak with us but most of the conversation consisted of smiles and nods our knowledge of French was of little use in a backwater of the Pyrénées.

A highlight of our week at the chateau was the village 'Jour de Fête'. To celebrate the feast-day of their patron saint all the villagers wore national costume, identical to that worn by St Bernadette. We attended High Mass in the village church, watched the display of national dancing in the square and, in the evening, were allowed to go to the dance that was held in the open air. The square was festooned with lanterns and the night was very hot; dripping with perspiration we were whirled around by the village lads for dance after dance until it was time to return to the chateau.

There were visits to the tiny market town of Laruns and walks with Mère Marie Thérèse de Jesus and the Convent dog, Partout. One day a small coach was hired to take us high into the mountains to the Lac d'Artouste just over the Spanish border. In contrast to the

French Pyrénées, the Spanish ones are parched and arid, and when we stopped for a picnic lunch we were reminded forcibly and feelingly of Hilaire Belloc's famous reference to 'the fleas that tease in the High Pyrénées'! In the afternoon the coach ascended to a great height in the mountains and there before us lay the Lac, breathtakingly lovely; we were able to ride around the lakeside on a mountain railtrack in open carriages.

After our week in Béost we took the train to Lourdes where we stayed for a night in a hotel. Unfortunately just before we were due to set off for the Torchlight Procession I had a major nose-bleed which showed no signs of stopping and the others reluctantly had to leave me behind. However, a kind French couple at the hotel took me under their wing, plugged me with wads of cotton wool and took me with them to the Domaine. We were too late for the Procession but I was taken to the Grotto and given some pure, cold, refreshing Lourdes water from the spring to drink. There, among the crowds of people, I was spotted by our party, pleased that I had been able to come to the Grotto after all. The visit to Lourdes was only brief, but I was to return many years later as one of the bluebereted Hand-Maids who help with the sick pilgrims.

On our way to Béost we had stopped for a few hours at Pau, where we had to change trains. Mother AElfreda took us to visit an old lady, a former 'ancienne éleve'. I remember a large room, very French, with velvet-covered chairs and sofas around the walls; the old lady seemed very much a 'grande dame'.

We were rather shy and on our best behaviour, somewhat awed by the formal atmosphere and having been well drilled beforehand about being careful to observe the 'convenances'. The 'grande dame' was very kind and gracious and served us with tea and small cakes, but we had had a long journey, sitting up all night in the train from Paris, the room was hot and stuffy and I had to struggle to keep my eyes open and my head from nodding; the visit seemed interminable!

The holiday was a most memorable and enjoyable one, as were all visits abroad with the nuns. On our last evening at the chateau we had entertained Mère Therese and Sister Catherine with our by then famous rendering of 'The Obstructive Hat'; we had forgotten some of the lines, but were adept at improvising. The visit to Béost had ended on a very happy note.

Chapter Twenty-Two

On returning from France I learnt that I had successfully passed School Certificate. So far there had not been a Sixth Form at Rise, and Mother AElfreda with her usual vision determined to start one. I had done sufficiently well in the examinations to warrant my following an academic career but there was my mother's opposition to be overcome. She had expected me to leave school at sixteen and take a secretarial course, and was very opposed to the notion that I should go to University. Mother AElfreda visited our house during the summer holidays to try to persuade her.

An hour's talking over a cup of tea finally resulted in success: I was to be allowed to stay on at school for a further two years and sit the Higher School Certificate. I learnt only later that the Convent had offered to waive the fees, as mother herself could not afford to keep me on at school.

It was decided that I should take English, French and History, with Latin subsidiary, the only problem being that I had dropped the latter subject in my School Certificate year and I needed a pass in it in order to gain exemption from Matriculation. In my first year in the sixth form (called A2 at the Convent) I was going to have to cram in order to take Latin School Certificate in the December whilst studying for it at subsidiary level.

The Convent had promised that, where they were unable to supply the necessary teaching, substitute tuition would be paid for by the school. This had, in fact, already been done in our School Certificate year, when an excellent teacher (whose name I have forgotten) came out to Rise each Thursday to teach us Maths for a whole afternoon; it was exhausting but was a welcome improvement on poor little Buggy's lessons. As soon as the autumn term began,

Maureen Matthews, who needed science for her chosen career of physiotherapy, went several times a week to the Hull Convent, and also the Technical College, for lessons (having to learn it all from scratch!) and I was sent into Hull twice a week for private tuition with a retired teacher, a former Latin master at the school my brother had attended many years previously Hymer's College. I forget the master's name but retain happy memories of the lessons I had with him. Rather like Mr Chips, he lived within sight of the College; unlike Mr Chips, he was very fierce! Surprisingly he didn't frighten me (perhaps because of a twinkle in his eye), and I believe he was surprised to find himself with a female pupil who was hardworking and who grasped things quickly. For the whole of that term I spent every spare minute memorising vocabulary, irregular verbs and conjugations, declensions and constructions until I knew the whole of Kennedy's Grammar by heart. I was very proud of the congratulatory card my fierce but likeable master sent me when I passed the examination with an 'A'.

Mother AElfreda took me for English, Loffy for French Language, and Buggy took me for Latin and had an attempt at teaching me French Literature; in the end I studied that subject for myself with the help of books from the University Library for which Mother AElfreda, as a former student, had a reader's ticket. Brenda Hastings and I, who were both taking History, went into Hull twice a week for lessons with a master from Hull Grammar School. He, like my Latin master, was an excellent teacher as was Miss Layton, an artist who taught at the Convent and to whom we had been sent for lessons before sitting for the School Certificate.

Once we had moved to Rise, the nuns could not be faulted in the teaching provision they gave us. Later, after we had left school, two former classrooms were turned into laboratories and Mrs Cromwell came out from Hull to teach Science. Elizabeth Cromwell had had a long association with the Convent; she had been at school with my sister and as a child I knew her as Bessie Holme. The association was further reinforced when her daughter Anne became a pupil at Rise, as did so many other children of former pupils.

My last two years at Rise were very full. As I was determined not to let the nuns down, and also because of the need to prove myself to my mother, I worked very hard at my studies. In addition, I had been made Head Girl, with the responsibilities it entailed along with being a House Captain, and I had formed a small school choir which necessitated regular practices. Sentimental as ever, we entertained Reverend Mother and the Community with 'Bless this House', 'The Holy City', 'Vienna, City of my Dreams' and a rendering of Gounod's 'Ave Maria' with Philippa Greaves as the soloist. I was also involved in sport and had supervisory duties. When I was called upon to take Study or be in charge in the Refectory, I was able to sympathise with Loffy over the times we had tried her patience.

One term I was even a pupil-teacher! I was asked if I would teach Geography to one of the lower forms, as nobody else was available. I enjoyed it, although I don't know if my pupils did! They certainly behaved themselves, already having a healthy respect for my authority and (I have since learnt) regarding me with awe! One forgets how exalted Sixth Form pupils seem to eleven and twelve year olds.

A lot of time during the week was occupied in travelling back and forth from Hull on the bus, which cut down studying time. English, French and Latin Literature, on top of History, involved a great deal of reading and learning. As well as everything else I was, at Mother AElfreda's urging, studying for the Oxford Entrance Examination at the same time as for Higher School Certificate; this meant also having to take the extra Scholarship paper and reading as widely as possible.

At Matron's instigation I had been given a bedroom to share with Maureen Matthews, which served as a study during the day, and was allowed to go to bed later than the others. The last hour of the day was usually spent studying at a table in the Sick Bay, with Matron sometimes bringing me a hot drink. All this eventually began to tell; I was under immense pressure and suddenly developed blinding migraines.

One evening, on returning from a lesson in Hull, I was met at the front door by Mother AElfreda, who said Reverend Mother wanted me to help sing Mass at the Convent the next morning. Almost in tears from exhaustion I begged to be excused, but to no avail: I had to pack an overnight bag and return to Hull by the next bus! Reverend Mother's word was law.

Chapter Twenty-Three

It was a welcome relief from work to be able, in the Easter holidays of 1950, to go with a group of nuns, girls and Matron Nerny on a pilgrimage to Rome for the Holy Year. We stayed first of all at Meudon and then caught the Orient Express, which took us through Switzerland and Italy to Florence, our first stopping place.

The journey was long and uncomfortable, because we travelled third class and had to sleep as best we could sitting upright, but we were thrilled by the sight of Lake Geneva the next morning, and even more so by Florence where we were to stay for a few days.

It is hard to say which comes first in my memory: the wonderful architecture, sculptures, paintings and frescoes we saw, or the great embarrassment of suddenly finding my silk camiknickers around my ankles. As with most of my clothes, they had belonged to my sister, handsewn by her and beautifully stitched, a credit to the nuns who had taught her. Unfortunately they were held up by only a button, which had worked loose; down they came, right in the middle of one of the most famous streets. To my relief Reverend Mother was walking ahead of us and missed seeing the incident (but she was of course told of it and teased me about it at lunch). Had she witnessed it she would perhaps have been proud of the presence of mind with which I stepped out of the knickers, quickly picked them up and stuffed them into the bag carried by Philippa Greaves who was walking beside me. I hoped not too many people had noticed!

That incident took place on our way back from the Pitti Palace. Magnificent as the latter was, I was even more appreciative of the Convent of San Marco. I was studying Byron at the time for Higher School Certificate, and his 'Fra Lippo Lippi' came alive for me when we saw that famous artist's frescoes on the walls around the cloister.

We walked across the Ponte Vecchio and gazed at the River Arno, significant for us because of Joan Hammond's recording of 'Oh, my beloved father' which was popular at the time. We also learnt how to barter with the many vendors who tried to sell us their wares. We thought there could be no place more beautiful than Florence.

On the way to Rome we spent a day at Assisi and loved its steep, narrow, winding streets, up which the laden donkeys struggled doggedly. We walked down the road from the town to the Portziuncula, the tiny chapel used by St Francis around which a church had been built; we saw the Convent of St Clare and were impressed by the Basilica of St Francis. On a decidedly less spiritual note, the day was highlighted by an incident outside the Basilica. A coach had drawn up and disgorged its occupants; suddenly Matron told us not to look. Naturally we disobeyed and saw a row of priests (or maybe Seminarians) urinating against a wall! The visit to Italy was educational in more ways than one.

In contrast to that display of 'insouciance' we were amused, at the hotel where we had lunch, by the lengths that were gone to in order to disguise from us the fact that Reverend Mother needed to go to the lavatory. When she left the dining-room before us we were told not to look, and were bidden to stay away from the cloakroom for a little while. The nuns had been dispensed from the rule which forbade them to eat in public, but that was as far as things could go in the days of pre-Vatican Two.

Florence was beautiful but Rome, we found, was in another realm; it was magnificent. We had only four days there, but that was sufficient for us to absorb and appreciate the historical significance both pagan and religious. The size of St Peter's amazed us; it was difficult to believe the evidence that Westminster Abbey was three times smaller than that great Basilica and could have been turned right round inside it. We could not have envisaged, either, the size of the crowd who had waited inside and out for the Audience with Pope Pius the Twelfth. To see his small, white-cassocked figure borne aloft on the Sedia Gestatoria through the cheering mass of people was moving and unforgettable. Unforgettable too were the indescribably beautiful Pieta, sculpted in white marble by Michelangelo, and the huge bronze statue of St Peter, one of his toes almost worn away by the countless generations of pilgrims who had knelt to kiss it.

Inside the Vatican there was a feast of art to gaze upon: the ceiling of the Sistine Chapel, the famous painting of the Last Supper, countless paintings by Raphael. Wherever we went in Rome, we came face to face with the originals of the Great Masters whose works we had previously seen only in books; it was wonderful to see the Venus de Milo and Michelangelo's flawless sculpture of David. It came almost as a relief to be brought down to earth for a while when we were taken to a church in a side street and descended to the crypt. We had witnessed immortality in art form: now we were confronted with human mortality; the crypt was piled high with the skulls and skeletons of generations of monks. It was a gruesome sight but also a forcible reminder that Rome had been the centre of Christianity for almost two thousand years. The piles of bones reached far back into the past.

In Florence we had encountered the Renaissance; in Rome I understood the meaning and significance of 'Classical'. We were truly transported into history, walking not only where St Peter had trod but also able to relive scenes of Ancient Rome. Paganism, mythology and the Roman Emperors were juxtaposed with Christianity, with scenes from the Acts of the Apostles, and with martyrdom. Truth and legend existed side by side. We gazed, bereft of words, at the dungeon where St Peter had been imprisoned; when we stood in the ancient Forum, Shakespeare's 'Julius Caesar' was brought to life. In the Colosseum we saw in our imagination the early Christians being thrown to the lions; we obeyed custom and climbed on our knees the long flight of the Holy Steps, up which Jesus was said to have walked before his Crucifixion. We went underground through the maze of Catacombs, the ancient Roman burial place made holy by the early Christians who had sought shelter and lived there to escape persecution; we walked along the Appian Way to the spot where St Peter, fleeing from persecution in Rome, is said to have had a vision of Christ 'Quo vadis?' asked St Peter. 'Where are you going?' 'I am going to Rome to be crucified a second time,' said Jesus, and in shame Peter turned back to face his own martyrdom.

It seemed incredible that in Rome we were actually treading on the ground where history had been made. The Eternal City had us in thrall and we threw a coin into the Trevi Fontana to ensure that one day we would return.

The four packed days came to an end too soon. As it happened, it was as well, for Mother AElfreda became ill on the last day, when we were inside one of the churches after hearing Mass. It was the start of a nervous breakdown. Somehow she survived the long and arduous journey back but she was ill for most of the next term, the one leading up to my Higher School Certificate, managing only to give me a few lessons up in her room.

Chapter Twenty-Four

Adult memories of long, hot summers are usually treated with scepticism, but when I was studying for my exams there were certainly heatwaves and I have snapshots to prove it. Much of my swotting was done in the garden sitting under the shade of one of the magnificent trees there. (Substantiated rumour has it that Mother Hilda was once spotted perched on a lower branch of a tree, reading her breviary; such was the delightful unconventionality of our nuns.)

On summer evenings whilst others were in Study I walked around the perimeters, notebook in hand, learning by heart the carefully résuméd facts I had compiled, or memorising lists of French and Latin vocabulary; each day I set myself a target of learning new facts and new words, after mentally revising those already learnt. One of the distinct advantages of being at a boarding school was that we were able to study in quiet, congenial surroundings and build up a habit of concentration; another was that our teachers were mostly on hand outside school hours, should we need to ask questions or seek further help.

Sometimes I took the narrow path that led to the village church, or walked in the park hardly noticing the curious stares of the cattle that grazed there, I was so immersed. I did, however, take care to avoid the bull, remembering a walk we had once been on with Loffy, when we had all been obliged to run for our lives and clamber over a barbed wire fence. Loffy was afraid of cattle but on that occasion her fear was justified!

Summers at Rise meant that ties were discarded, and the open sash windows on the ground floor provided a much quicker means of egress to the garden than having to go down a corridor and out through the side door. This unorthodox and unladylike behaviour was frowned upon but not expressly forbidden. When the windows were open, lessons were accompanied by the humming of bees and the cooing of wood pigeons; to this day, these sounds are for me evocative of Rise, as is the heady perfume of mock orange blossom, a scent which wafted in through the windows and pervaded the chapel, where huge bunches of the blossom had been placed.

In summer too, groups of children could be seen squatting on the cobbles in the stable courtyard, or on the gravelled paths, engaged in pulling up the ever-encroaching weeds. This was the normal and much-hated punishment meted out by the HouseCaptains to young offenders.

Frequently a small figure was spotted walking through the grounds, calling 'Perdi, Perdi, Perdi?' That was little Buggy looking for her cat; she had given it the Latin name of Perdita because she was always losing it. At other times Mother Aloysia could be seen in her blue apron, skirts tucked up, wheeling a wheelbarrow as she went about her voluntary task of fighting the weeds in the garden. There is one picture that will always be etched on the minds of my contemporaries: that of Loffy coming into the garden ringing a large brass handbell to summon us in from recreation.

The time came for me to leave school and its familiar sights and sounds. I was eighteen, had sat my Higher School Certificate (but failed the Oxford Entrance,) had been accepted at Hull University College- then attached to the University of London- and was of an age to be launched into the adult world. I had been doubly one of the pioneers at Rise and, after I left, the school went from strength to strength, with others succeeding in the Oxford Entrance Exam where I had failed.

During my final year at the Convent we had undergone an Inspection. The school was totally Independent, unattached in any way to the state educational system and with no irksome bureaucratic red-tape. It was felt, however, that the time had come to seek Recognition. During the inspection we put on our best showing, determined not to let the nuns down, and I remember saving Buggy's bacon during a Latin setbook lesson when she and I were visited by one of the inspectors- a kindly, venerable old man. Despite my earlier success, Latin did not come easily to me and I needed to make good use of a crib when learning the setbooks. Sitting at Buggy's side at the large, round, antique table that served as a teacher's desk, the inspector seated at a school desk a few yards away, I fluently and effortlessly translated the Caesar in front of me (reading from the crib!) and the inspector was suitably impressed; at the same time I earned Mother Aloysia's gratitude! It was cheating, perhaps, but for a good cause; Rise was granted Recognition, and the excellent academic record the school was later to achieve justified this.

On my last evening at school I was given a grand farewell dinner, beautifully laid out on the long refectory table in the library and served by the nuns (who had even provided a bottle of wine.) I had come a long way from my early beginnings at Boynton, when I had been shy, awkward and uncertain of myself; I had learnt to exercise authority, show initiative and have self-respect and dignity. That dignity did not prevent me, though, from still climbing out of the classroom window as a quicker means of exit than through the side door! Life with the nuns had taught us to be well balanced.

The next morning my mother, driven by my brother in our firm's van, came to collect me. I departed in floods of tears!

It was the end of my schooldays and childhood, though not of my connection with Rise for the umbilical cord was never severed. A new life was once again about to begin.

CONCLUSION

'Plus çà Change...'

Changes are inevitable, and many such gradually took place after I left school the interior of the Hall was at last redecorated; semi-derelict outbuildings were turned into classrooms or labs; the number of day-girls and lay-staff increased; the boarders were allowed to change out of uniform after school hours; the grounds became well-cared for, and attractive flower-beds were laid out under the tender care of Mère Marie de l'Annunciation (affectionately known as Nuncy) and there was not a weed to be seen in the cobbled courtyard; finally came the longed for gymnasium and hall. All that was for the good.

Other changes were indicative of the times: younger Old Girls reminisce about having placed bets on the Grand National, and Jill Armstrong, Editor of the Woman's Page of the Yorkshire Post, has recalled how two of them lowered a basket of food to a group of miscreants who, having been caught smoking, had been put in detention in their classroom for a long period which presumably included involuntary fasting! At the time when my generation of pupils entered the school we were more innocent: smoking was not a temptation and we certainly had no access to betting shops! However, we were by no means angelic and I myself have since made up for those particular omissions!

Changes at Rise there were but two familiar aspects never altered: the plastic buckets placed at strategic spots where the roof leaked, and (apart from a brief disruptive period) the wonderfully happy atmosphere.

The education we received at the hands of the nuns was based firmly on the principles of love, friendliness, kindness, inclusiveness, gentleness and truth. Education is essentially development and formation, and we were encouraged to develop our own individuality; at the same time characters were formed almost imperceptibly along the lines of Christian principles and values. The régime was not a 'soft' one; on the contrary, it strengthened our characters but did so without having the effect of making us hard. Such a formation makes for vulnerability but it ensures the retention of integrity.

I believe that what characterises the majority both of nuns and former pupils is spontaneity, the capacity for enjoyment, a balanced approach to life and religion, and a lack of falsity and affectation. It is such qualities that make for the homogeneous harmony that exists among us when we come together.

Some people may, on reading what has been written, be tempted to quote Shakespeare's well-known line: 'Methinks the lady doth protest too much!' Perhaps the emphasis I have laid on the form of education we received is the result of strong disagreement with a speaker I heard on the radio one day. He scornfully rejected the part that Christianity may have to play in schools, and claimed that Humanism too teaches morality. My belief is that morality and true Christianity are not necessarily one and the same; the former can be cold and unforgiving, whereas the latter is characterised by warmth and acceptance. That was the main reason for Sarah Bernhardt's love affair with Grand-Champs and that same reason holds good for the pupils who passed through the nuns' hands at Hull, Boynton and Rise.

Although as pupils we attended an Independent School, in many ways we did not lead a privileged life, and my generation at least certainly lacked most of the school facilities others regard as necessary for a good education. We were, however, privileged to have had a truly Christian upbringing. There I rest my case! I doubt whether many former pupils will dispute it.

POSTCRIPT

Sadly in 1989 Rise Hall ceased to exist as a school, for it was no longer financially viable. For the many former pupils who came together for the final Mass there on July 8th the occasion was one of great sorrow and regret, despite the happiness of joyful reunions and shared reminiscence. Many of us wondered why it was called a 'Celebration Mass', but after hearing the homily preached by Bishop Harris we began to understand the reason: we had come together in thanksgiving for the education we had all received at Rise, and for the spirit by which it was characterised. That spirit will remain alive, because it will be passed on among former pupils, from parents and teachers to the children in their care.

Members of the Old Girls' Association retain their link with their former school through the twice yearly News Letter that Sister Geraldine so kindly takes the trouble to compile, as well as through the regular Reunions. Through these we hear news of the Community and of former pupils.

The following quotations from the News Letter of March 1994, to which Old Girls of all ages sent news of themselves, need no further comment:

"I have so many happy memories of Rise...I dug up a little clump of aconites (from the grounds.) As they spread I put some in my mother's garden, then some in Lorraine's, so now we all have a little bit of Rise every spring."

"Until a small lab was set up at Rise in the mid 1950's, the Rise biologists had to travel into Hull weekly by bus for their lessons. My mother was delighted when she was able to start visiting Rise instead and always had a particular affection for the Rise atmosphere which, she firmly believed, bred independent-minded and resourceful people!"

"I was no academic and found spelling tortuous...Mother Hilda once said, 'Never mind, dear, Winifred Holtby had difficulty with spelling but she did write *South Riding*."

"When my eldest child was five, I decided I needed to return to education. I was truly bitten by the Rise bug!...It was really great to see Joyce this summer. I invited myself to her house when I visited Rise. She remembered me immediately as if it was yesterday. I was amazed."

"I only spent two years at Rise. They were precious years. I loved Mother AElfreda dearly; she made me feel a part of the family. I was reassured when I returned unexpectedly this summer. We were all made to feel welcome. Long Live Rise!"

It is perhaps fitting to end with the final words of the Bishop's sermon, which was one of optimism:

"A school is people. A Christian school is people passing on Christian joy from generation to generation. And so a school can never die. A school which proclaims the Gospel is an Easter school. The death of its structures can never kill its message. So we give thanks for all that Rise Hall School has done and given in the past. And we give thanks for all that Rise Hall School will do in the years ahead."

AMEN.

ACKNOWLEDGEMENTS

I am grateful to Ruth Brandon for permission to quote from her biography of Sarah Bernhardt, *Being Divine*, together with the publishers, Martin Secker & Warburg Ltd; also to Sister Geraldine, Vicar Provincial, for her encouragement and for the loan of photographs, and Sister Alexia for lending prints and helping in numerous ways.

In addition I am indebted to those former pupils who were able to jog my memory and to supply a few reminiscences of their own, in particular Maureen Matthews, June Davies (née Tong), the former Walker twins Betty Biggs and Hilary Thornton, and Jill Armstrong who allowed me to make use of an article she published in the *Yorkshire Post*.